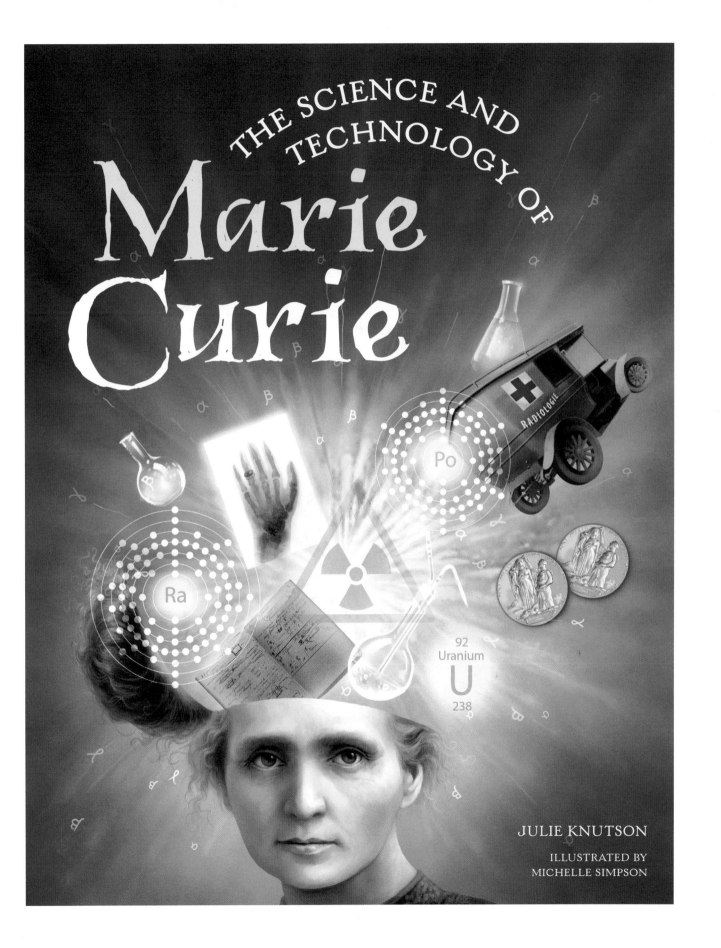

THE SCIENCE AND TECHNOLOGY OF
Marie Curie

Po

RADIOLOGIE

Ra

92
Uranium
U
238

JULIE KNUTSON

ILLUSTRATED BY
MICHELLE SIMPSON

Titles in the **Build It Yourself Science Biographies** Set

Check out more titles at www.nomadpress.net

Nomad Press

A division of Nomad Communications

10 9 8 7 6 5 4 3 2 1

This book was manufactured by Versa Press, East Peoria, Illinois
June 2021, Job #1019926
ISBN Softcover: 978-1-64741-022-3
ISBN Hardcover: 978-1-64741-019-3

Educational Consultant, Marla Conn

Questions regarding the ordering of this book should be addressed to
Nomad Press
PO Box 1036, Norwich, VT 05055
www.nomadpress.net

Printed in the United States.

CONTENTS

Interested in Primary Sources? Look for this icon.

Use a smartphone or tablet app to scan the QR code and explore more! Photos are also primary sources because a photograph takes a picture at the moment something happens. You can find a list of URLs on the Resources page. If the QR code doesn't work, try searching the internet with the Keyword Prompts to find other helpful sources.

🔎 Marie Curie

May 15, 1859: Pierre Curie is born in Paris, France.

November 7, 1867: Marie Skłodowska is born in Warsaw, Poland.

1869: In Russia, Dimitri Mendeleev publishes the first periodic table of elements, featuring the 63 elements known at the time.

1882: Marie begins learning in secret at Warsaw's Flying University.

1891: After seven years of working as a governess to fund her elder sister's education, Marie moves to Paris to attend the Sorbonne.

1893: Marie completes her degree in physics, finishing first among graduates. The next year, she earns another degree in mathematics.

July 26, 1895: Marie and fellow scientist Pierre Curie wed in a garden ceremony. The couple celebrate their honeymoon with an extended bike riding holiday.

1897: Marie Curie investigates physicist Henri Becquerel's findings on uranium salts. Soon, Pierre joins in her work.

September 12, 1897: Marie Curie gives birth to daughter Irène in Paris.

1898: Marie and Pierre Curie announce the discovery of two new elements, polonium and radium. The Curies coin the term *radioactivity* to describe the properties of these elements.

June 1903: Marie Curie becomes the first woman to earn a PhD from the Sorbonne.

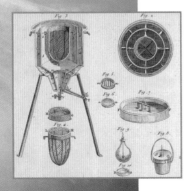

December 1903: The Curies share the Nobel Prize in physics with Henri Becquerel. Initially, Marie Curie is left off of the nomination. Her name is added after objections from Pierre and other scientists.

December 6, 1904: The Curies welcome their second daughter, Ève, in Paris.

April 19, 1906: Pierre dies in a traffic accident in Paris.

May 1906: Curie becomes the first female professor in the history of the Sorbonne.

December 1911: Curie wins the Nobel Prize in chemistry. She remains the only person to win two Nobel Prizes in two sciences.

1914–1918: Curie organizes mobile radiology units for French forces during World War I. X-ray units coordinated by Curie's team are used on more than 1 million soldiers during the conflict.

May–June 1921: Marie Curie travels to the United States to collect a gram of radium, crowdsourced by American women, for her institute.

October 1929: Curie makes a second trip to the United States to collect another gram of radium, this time for use at the Curie Institute in Warsaw.

July 4, 1934: Curie dies in Savoy, France, at the age of 66. She is buried alongside her husband, Pierre.

1935: Irène Joliot-Curie and her husband, Jean Frédéric Joliot-Curie, are awarded the Nobel Prize in chemistry for their discovery of artificial radioactivity.

1995: The remains of Marie Curie and her husband are reinterred in the Panthéon in Paris alongside other notable French citizens. She is the first woman to be buried in the monument.

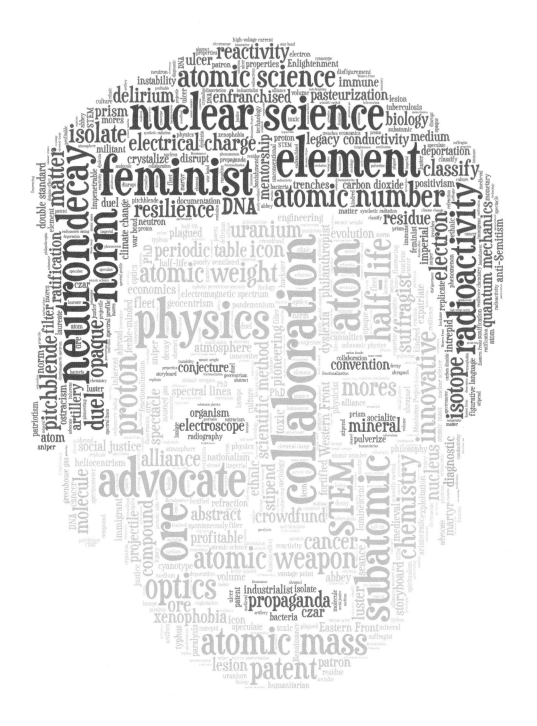

MEET
MARIE CURIE

During the late 1800s and early 1900s, a handful of scientists tirelessly worked to bring about a huge shift in scientific knowledge. They wanted to prove that everything we are and everything we see is made up of tiny parts, smaller than anything humans had ever imagined.

And at the forefront of this group of **intrepid** science pioneers was an unlikely figure who defied **convention** to reset the way that scientists work. She laid the foundations for the new field of **atomic science**.

Her name was Marie Skłodowska Curie (1867–1934).

ESSENTIAL QUESTION

How does scientific knowledge change through time?

WORDS TO KNOW

intrepid: fearless or adventurous.

convention: the way things are usually done.

atomic science: the field of science that studies the structure of **atoms**, the arrangement of their particles, and how these arrangements can change.

atom: a very small piece of matter. Atoms are the tiny building blocks that combine to make up everything in the universe.

WORDS TO KNOW

disrupt: to make a major disturbance that interrupts the usual order of things.

chemistry: the science of how atoms and **molecules** combine to form substances and how those substances interact, combine, and change.

molecule: a group of atoms bound together. Molecules combine to form matter.

physics: the study of physical forces, including matter, energy, and motion, and how these forces interact with each other.

biology: the study of life and living things.

matter: anything that has weight and takes up space. Almost everything is made of matter.

norm: something that is typical or standard.

element: a basic substance, such as gold or oxygen, made of only one kind of atom.

Imagine the world of science as a city in the heart of a region known for its massive earthquakes. There are periods of quiet, periods of tremor, and moments of violent, earth-shaking rattling. During these rare, groundbreaking instances, thousand-page books tumble from shelves. Chairs and tables get turned over by invisible energy. Giant canyons split open the planet's surface.

After these massive quakes—even when the books are reshelved and the tables and chairs are righted—the land is fundamentally changed. Every person sees the world differently.

Why? Because of scientific discovery. In science, these dramatic shifts are driven by people and teams of people working, building upon, **disrupting**, and reshaping how we think about the surrounding world and even how we live in it.

Just more than a century ago, scientists were furiously working on a project to break down the seen into the unseen. Investigators in the emerging fields of **chemistry**, **physics**, and **biology** were part of a 2,000-year-old detective story that aimed to solve a critical mystery: What tiny pieces combine to make us? What tiny pieces make up the **matter** that makes up everything else in the universe?

Marie Curie was a scientist leading the way in discovering the answers to these questions.

Marie Curie around 1920
Credit: Henri Manuel

MEET MARIE

Marie Skłodowska was the last of five children born to educator parents in Warsaw, Poland, in 1867. Throughout her life, her drive to understand the world around her gave her the courage to reset social rules and **norms**.

In 1891, at age 24, she left Poland to study in Paris, France. She earned degrees in physics and mathematics and went on to conduct scientific research that shattered people's perceptions and world views.

Despite living in a time and place that offered very LIMITED OPPORTUNITIES for women, Marie persisted in HER QUEST FOR KNOWLEDGE.

During her early career as a scientist, she partnered with her husband, Pierre Curie (1859–1906). The pair met in 1894 and married the following year. Together, they labored in a shoddy lab to uncover the mysteries of matter. They managed to beat the odds and identify two new **elements**: radium and polonium. For this contribution to science, they were awarded a Nobel Prize. They also had two daughters, Irène (1897–1956) and Ève (1904–2007). Irène won a Nobel Prize of her own in 1935.

Marie and Pierre Curie with Irène at their home near Paris, France, c. 1900

WORDS TO KNOW

radioactivity: the emission of energy in the form of a stream of particles or electromagnetic rays.

cancer: a disease caused by the uncontrolled dividing of abnormal cells in one's body.

technology: the tools, methods, and systems used to solve a problem or do work.

geocentrism: the belief, now disproved, that the earth is the center of the solar system.

heliocentrism: the belief that the sun is the center of the solar system.

radiography: the process of taking radiographs, similar to X-rays, to assist in medical examinations.

After Pierre Curie tragically died in a 1906 street accident, Marie continued their shared effort to better understand **radioactivity**. She investigated possible applications in treating diseases, such as **cancer**. During World War I, she used science and **technology** to help wounded soldiers.

Ultimately, she sacrificed her own life for her work. Years of handling and testing radioactive substances wore her body down.

Today, Marie Curie remains one of the most recognized figures in the history of science.

Changemakers in Science

Every generation seems to experience a kind of scientific revolution, some larger than others. For example, for a very long time, people thought that the sun revolved around the earth. This human, earth-centered view—called **geocentrism**—was favored for thousands of years. Then, during the 1500s, Nicolaus Copernicus (1473–1543) came up with a mathematical model that demonstrated **heliocentrism**. In 1610, Galileo Galilei (1564–1642) used telescopes to strengthen Copernicus' theory and disprove geocentrism. What might it have been like for people to suddenly have to rethink their model of the entire universe?

In recent decades, a digital revolution has dramatically altered how we connect with each other and interact with the world. From the way people influence politics to how we communicate with distant relatives to how we attend school, few aspects of life have gone untouched by computerized technology. How is this similar to Curie's time?

BREAKING SCIENTIFIC AND SOCIAL BARRIERS

The Nobel Prize is an annual prize in the sciences, literature, medicine, and peace, which was established by Alfred Nobel (1833–1896) more than a century ago. Marie Curie was the first woman awarded a Nobel Prize—and not just once, but twice. She earned them in less than a decade. She was the first woman to earn a degree in physics at the famous university in Paris called the Sorbonne, the first appointed a professorship at the same institution, and the first—in its 224-year history—elected to the French Academy of Medicine.

Marie Curie's life was governed by the motto, "SCIENCE IN THE SERVICE OF HUMANITY."

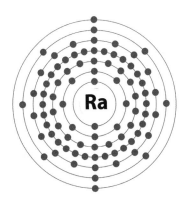

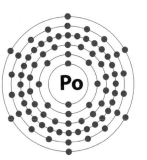

This amazing scientist discovered two elements, radium and polonium. She coined the term *radioactivity* and revolutionized how instruments were used in scientific experimentation. She pioneered medical applications of new technologies in cancer treatment and **radiography**.

WORDS TO KNOW

innovative: coming up with new ideas or methods of doing things.

sociology: the study of human relationships and social problems.

philosophy: the study of truth, wisdom, the nature of reality, and knowledge.

isolate: to separate one thing from another.

ore: a naturally occurring mineral that contains metal.

culture: the beliefs and way of life of a group of people, which can include religion, language, art, clothing, food, and holidays.

physicist: a scientist who studies physics.

economics: having to do with the resources and wealth of a country and the material welfare of humankind.

mores: the customs and conventions of a community.

vantage point: a place or position showing a view of something.

In the history of science, Marie Curie matters because of her quest to make the invisible visible. In her lab work, she approached scientific questions in **innovative** ways with new tools and technologies. In the process, she showed that invisible rays give off extraordinary energy from elemental substances. She tirelessly worked to **isolate** substances from tons and tons of **ore**. This work would lead to the discovery of two new elements.

Historians of science study the way HUMAN UNDERSTANDING of the world changes as time passes. This career combines science, history, sociology, and philosophy to get to the who, what, when, where, why, and how of new discoveries about our universe.

In the history of **culture**, Curie matters because of her role as a groundbreaker. In her time, women were expected to lead quiet lives as wives and mothers and never venture into the spheres of science, business, and other pursuits. They were supposed to stay home and take care of people.

Marie Curie made women visible as intellectual and scientific changemakers. And she had to fight hard to gain that recognition.

Marie and Pierre Curie working in the lab
Credit: Wellcome Collection (CC BY 4.0)

Even after Curie finished her doctoral studies, she couldn't present her own findings before France's all-male Academy of Sciences. This was not an unusual situation at that time. Female peers working elsewhere in Europe, such as superstar **physicist** Lise Meitner (1878–1968), toiled in basements and snuck beneath lecture hall seats because women weren't allowed in the main corridors of power and knowledge.

Marie Curie studied things that were so small, they couldn't be seen! How? Through careful experimentation and observation. **Take a look at the importance of observation and seeing the unseen in this science experiment video!**

🔎 Science Sophie observations

Despite all of the obstacles blocking women such as Curie and Meitner, they persisted. They set the stage for future generations of women in science.

Paris During the Belle Époque

Marie Curie disembarked at Gare du Nord train station in Paris in 1891. The City of Light was then 20 years into a period known as the Belle Époque, or "beautiful era," which lasted from roughly 1871 until 1941. What was so beautiful about this time? What made it distinct and unique? It was a time of transformation, with many changes in technology, **economics**, social **mores**, politics, and the arts. It was the time of the Second Industrial Revolution, when innovations in steel, chemical discoveries, the use of petroleum, and the development of electricity ushered in a totally new period in human history. Ever-taller structures such as the Eiffel Tower offered a new **vantage point** on the world. For the first time since the dawn of humankind, the darkness of night was lit up by a force other than fire— electric lights! Goods were produced on a mass scale and distributed globally through new means of transportation, including the steam engine. Chemical discoveries allowed a moment to be captured on film as the first cameras came into being. It was a period of disruption and change. It led many to rethink the world as they knew it and to experiment with new ways of living in it.

Lise Meitner

During the early twentieth century in France, Austria, and Germany, women's education typically ended at age 14. For the incredibly studious and science-minded Lise Meitner, this was unacceptable. As a child, Meitner slept with a notebook filled with detailed scientific observations beneath her pillow. When her traditional schooling ended, she began working with a private tutor. She finished eight years of coursework in just two years and went on to Vienna University, where she earned her doctoral degree in physics in 1905. When she applied for a job with Marie Curie's lab in Paris, she was rejected. Instead, she took a volunteer position at Max Planck's Chemistry Institute in Berlin. There, she worked in the basement, separately from her male colleagues. She couldn't attend lectures and even had to walk to a hotel eight blocks away to use the restroom!

Meitner's career path changed in 1908, when the Prussian government started admitting women to universities. Her abilities and knowledge of radioactivity catapulted her to the head of a division at the Kaiser Wilhelm Institute in 1913. Meitner's later research in **nuclear science** led to breakthroughs in energy production and also paved the way for the development of **atomic weapons**.

Element 109 on the **periodic table** is named in her honor— meitnerium. Despite being nominated for the Nobel Prize 48 times for her contributions to chemistry and physics, she never won the award.

Lise Meitner, 1906

In this book, we'll discover how Marie Curie reset scientific and social norms. What shaped her young mind when she was a child and young adult? What did she discover, how did she reach her findings, and why were these findings so groundbreaking for scientists? What was her lasting **legacy** and influence?

Let's begin then, in Poland, in 1867.

WORDS TO KNOW

nuclear science: the study of atoms.

atomic weapon: a powerful weapon that uses the energy released by the splitting of atoms.

periodic table: the chart that shows and organizes all the known elements.

legacy: the lasting influence of a person or event.

scientific method: the process scientists use to ask questions and do experiments to try to prove their ideas.

Good Science Practices

Every good scientist keeps a science journal! Scientists use the **scientific method** to keep their experiments organized. Choose a notebook to use as your science journal. As you read through this book and do the activities, keep track of your observations and record each step in a scientific method worksheet, like the one shown here.

Question: What are we trying to find out? What problem are we trying to solve?

Research: What is already known about the problem?

Hypothesis/Prediction: What do we think the answer will be?

Equipment: What supplies are we using?

Method: What procedure are we following?

Results: What happened? Why?

Each chapter of this book begins with an essential question to help guide your exploration of Marie Curie and her work. Keep the question in your mind as you read the chapter. At the end of each chapter, use your science journal to record your thoughts and answers.

ESSENTIAL QUESTION

How does scientific knowledge change through time?

EIFFEL TOWER

Built in 1889 for the World Exposition, the Eiffel Tower honored the French Revolution. It also showcased national engineering and design expertise to an audience of global visitors. Originally intended as a temporary monument, it remains one of the world's most visited landmarks.

The structure of the tower itself is actually quite simple! To understand how its rivets and beams join, build a model of your own.

Take a look at how the Eiffel Tower was built in this animated video. What do you note about the different stages of construction?

🔎 Eiffel Tower timelapse

❯ **First, look at photographs of the Eiffel Tower. What shapes do you see?** What do you notice about its base? How would you describe the structure?

❯ **With those observations in mind, assemble your structure.** Use toothpicks or spaghetti as pillars, beams, and platforms. Join them together with marshmallow rivets.

❯ **Experiment with a few different building techniques and with your materials.** What happens if you melt a marshmallow? What if you add other materials, such as tape or glue? What type of base makes for the strongest, highest tower?

Think Like Marie!

Why do inventors and innovators feel the need to put their successes on display, as in the case of the Eiffel Tower? How does invention and innovation bring societies together? Are these prominent displays ever bad for communities? Do some more research on the Eiffel Tower and think about its cultural role in addition to its role as a symbol of great engineering.

WORDS TO KNOW

engineering: the use of science, math, and creativity to design and build things.

*TEXT TO **WORLD***

Do you think there are more female or male scientists working today?

Chapter 1

THE MAKING OF A
MIND

At age 4, Marie Salomea Skłodowska—later known to the world as Marie Curie—stood before the locked doors of a glass cabinet filled with wonders. She admired the tubes, scales, **minerals**, and gold-leaf **electroscope** resting on its shelves.

The scientific tools in this glass cabinet belonged to her father, Professor Wladyslaw Skłodowski. They'd been unused for years. Why? After an 1863 uprising against **imperial** Russia, the city of Warsaw, Poland, where the family lived, came under increasingly strict rule. Polish scientists, including Marie's father, were no longer allowed to teach physics and chemistry or to hold positions in laboratories.

ESSENTIAL QUESTION

How did Marie Curie's early environment shape her as a scientist?

WORDS TO KNOW

mineral: a naturally occurring solid found in rocks and in the ground. Rocks are made of minerals. Gold and diamonds are precious minerals.

electroscope: an instrument that detects and measures electricity.

imperial: relating to an empire.

classify: to arrange by groups.

atomic mass: the mass, or the amount of physical matter, in an atom.

reactivity: the measure of how easily a substance undergoes a chemical reaction and releases energy.

conductivity: the measure of how easily a substance, or material, conducts electricity.

A Note on Names

Some authors list Marie Curie's birth name as Maria Salomea Skłodowska, while others settle on a different spelling, Marya Salomee. During her childhood, family and friends called her by her nickname, "Manya." Later, when she went to college in Paris, she registered as a student under the French name, Marie. And when she married Pierre Curie in 1895, Skłodowska changed to Curie.

A gold-leaf electroscope, 1878

But Russian efforts to block Polish people from learning wouldn't hold within the walls of this home! Marie's parents were both educators, and they were committed to developing their children's talents.

In this family, questions, debates, and thoughtful reflection were expected. A strong sense of pride and Polish identity was secretly nurtured. Their curious children—especially Marie—dreamed of the day when they could put these scientific tools to full use.

THE PURSUIT OF LEARNING

Marie Skłodowska, nicknamed "Manya" by family and friends, was born on November 7, 1867. The youngest of five children, she had no trouble keeping up with her older siblings.

At age 4, to the total surprise of everyone around her, she read her first words. Marie looked on as her older sister, Bronya, struggled to read a passage. She picked up the very same book and read the first sentence clearly and confidently. When she saw the shocked faces of her parents and sister, she burst into tears and apologized, "I didn't mean to do it . . . but it was so easy."

Wladyslaw Skłodowski and his daughters, Maria, Bronya, and Helena

Have a Seat at the Table!

Have you seen the periodic table? Hung on classroom walls, printed on textbook pages, and silkscreened on T-shirts, the periodic table is one of the most recognizable and universal tools in science. In 1869, when Marie was just 2 years old, Russian scientist Dimitri Mendeleev (1834–1907) published his periodic table, a system for **classifying** the known elements. Mendeleev's table provided a visual map of increasing **atomic mass**. It also showed that certain elements shared characteristics, such as **reactivity** or **conductivity**. This allowed them to be grouped into "families." According to his calculations, these qualities reoccurred at "periodic" intervals of seven—today, it is known that they repeat on eight intervals. In Mendeleev's time, there were 63 known elements. Because of the patterns and relationships he identified based on predicted mass and characteristics, spaces were built in for yet-to-be-discovered elements. Throughout the rest of the century, other chemists raced to fill in these spaces.

Watch this fun video about the periodic table.

🔎 Twas the Night Before the Periodic Table

WORDS TO KNOW

patriotism: a feeling of pride for one's country or homeland.

ethnic: a group sharing a common national or cultural tradition.

czar: the leader of imperial Russia.

aristocratic: of the highest social class or rank.

social justice: justice in access to wealth, opportunities, and privileges.

In Marie's hometown of Warsaw, learning was strictly controlled by the Russian authorities. To stamp out Polish **patriotism**, Polish-language learning was banned. School lessons were taught in Russian. **Ethnically** Polish students weren't allowed to learn their own history or read their own literature, and students were expected to pledge loyalty to Russia's **czar.**

Still, clever teachers and students preserved their language, history, and culture through a disguised curriculum. Polish history? That was listed as botany on the school schedule. Polish literature? Also known as German studies! When Russian officials came to observe classes, everyone knew to hide their secret classes.

In school, the student called upon to recite before a monitoring government visitor was nearly always Marie. Afterward, she always felt like a traitor to her Polish roots.

Warsaw between 1882 and 1888

Marie's parents were among those clever teachers doing what they could to keep learning alive. Her mother, Bronislawa, was the head of an all-girls school. This role wasn't common for women in Russian-ruled Poland, where higher learning was largely restricted to men.

Marie's father, a trained scientist, lost his job because of his pro-Polish views. To support their family of five, the parents made the choice to turn their home into a school. With 20 boarding students living in their house, the Skłodowski kids slept on couches to make room for the resident pupils.

Learning happened at every turn. Sunrise and sunsets allowed for science lessons about the earth's rotation. Storytime involved reading the works of Charles Dickens in one language and translating it into Polish along the way. The children and their parents thought about **social justice**, too, discussing inequality in women's education around the dinner table. The uniting family value was the pursuit of knowledge.

Once a mighty kingdom, **POLAND** was divided up in 1795 by Prussia, the **AUSTRIAN EMPIRE**, and the **RUSSIAN EMPIRE**. Warsaw, **Marie's hometown, fell under Russian authority. Many aristocratic** families, including the Skłodowskis, lost their land and fortunes under their new rulers.

WORDS TO KNOW

tuberculosis (TB): an infectious bacterial disease that often infects the lungs.

typhus: an often-fatal disease spread by lice, ticks, mites, and fleas.

positivism: the nineteenth-century philosophy that emphasized the scientific method, logic, and reason.

deportation: to send away or expel from a country.

THE DEMONS OF DISEASE

Throughout Marie's childhood, her mother battled **tuberculosis (TB).** Bronislawa tried to shield her children from the disease, using separate plates and avoiding physical contact. She even sought treatment in Austria and France, taking along Marie's 10-year-old sister, Zosia, as a nurse and companion. But when Bronislawa and Zosia returned to Warsaw, they faced another disease in their overcrowded house filled with boarding students: **typhus**. Zosia got sick with typhus and died in 1876. Just two years later, TB claimed Marie's mother's life.

Following these losses, Marie became so depressed that a teacher suggested a break from school. But her father didn't agree. Instead, he enrolled her in an even more intense, Russian-run school. In 1883, she graduated first in her class. But what was a bright, curious, and ambitious young woman to do in a country where high school graduation meant the end of the educational road?

Marie needed a break. After years of studying to the point of exhaustion, she went to live with relatives in the countryside.

Fake tonics were peddled to people who hoped to find a cure for their illness.

Credit: Wellcome Images (CC BY 4.0)

During this carefree year, she read novels, picked berries, played games, went to parties, enjoyed winter sleigh rides, and sketched. Still, her father continued to send her math problems by letter, because even on an extended holiday, learning never stopped.

In the early 1800s, imperial Russian playing cards featured maps of conquered areas along with coats of arms and local costumes. **This card represents Poland.** Who do you think produced these cards? Why do you think they were created?

🔍 LOC Kingdom of Poland

PURSUING HIGHER EDUCATION

After a year away from the city, Marie returned to Warsaw. At age 16, she found that she wasn't alone in wanting to pursue higher education. Her elder sister, Bronya, also aimed for more. She wanted to be a doctor. The two girls linked up with a network of like-minded, lifelong learners through a secret school called the Flying University.

The Philosophy of Positivism

As a young adult, Marie's thoughts and actions were influenced by the philosophy of **positivism**. Positivists believed that all statements needed to be backed by firm evidence and solid reasoning and rooted in real-world observation. They also thought that improved education could lead to a better society. The makeshift school for peasant children that Marie created while working as a governess was rooted in this idea. So, too, was the Flying University.

Students at this free, secret school met under the cloak of darkness. They attended lectures and discussions led by volunteer teachers. Locations constantly moved in order to evade the Russian police, who forbade higher education for women. Science, politics, literature—throughout its history, the Flying University kept these topics alive for Marie, Bronya, and more than 1,000 others who risked arrest and **deportation** to keep learning.

WORDS TO KNOW

abroad: in a foreign country or land.

stipend: a small salary.

banishment: to send someone away from a country or place as an official punishment.

While the sisters studied in secret at the Flying University, one question lingered: How would they apply their knowledge in a country that didn't recognize women's right to learn and work? They knew that in order to fully realize their potential and find happiness, they'd have to seek formal education elsewhere.

Because the family didn't have the money to send both young women **abroad**, the two made a promise. Marie would stay in Poland and work as a governess to earn money to fund Bronya's medical studies in France. In turn, once Bronya earned her degree, she would send for Marie and pay for her schooling. Within a week, Marie went to work.

Marie was hired by the owner of a rural beet-sugar factory to tutor his children. She worked for them for three years, befriending the eldest daughter. Together, they even offered secret lessons in the family's kitchen to local children who couldn't afford school.

A School for High Fliers

The Flying University, sometimes called the Floating University, began in 1882. Leading intellectual figures in Warsaw launched the school, offering free classes to anyone who wanted to attend. Why did they start it? To provide a secret place for women to pursue education in Russian-occupied Poland. These intellectuals also wanted to give students a way to learn about Polish history and culture. The founders were motivated by the positivist belief that education and reasoned thought improved society. In their view, a better world could be built through empowering individuals through education. As time passed, the school grew. Small tuitions and fees allowed for a library to be built. Teachers were paid a small **stipend**. By the 1890s, men were attending, too, drawn by the accomplished faculty and high-quality courses. The school continued to operate secretly until 1905, when restrictions on education loosened.

This activity could have meant **banishment**, but Marie persisted. She was driven by the belief that societies improved if all people had access to education.

Her time with the family came to an ugly end when she and the eldest son fell in love. While the two wanted to marry, the wealthy farmer and his wife saw Marie as an unsuitable match. She returned to Warsaw and the Flying University as soon as her father got a new job that allowed him to shoulder the responsibility for Bronya's fees.

Back in Warsaw, Marie worked for another two years as a governess. At night and on weekends, she trained at one of the Flying University's illegal labs.

The Museum of Industry and Agriculture, where Marie Curie did some of her first work

WORDS TO KNOW

plagued: deeply troubled.

Within the walls of the Museum of Industry and Agriculture, Marie relished her time experimenting with physics and chemistry. Finally, she was working with the tubes, scales, minerals, and tools that she had admired as a 4-year-old, looking up at her father's glass case of instruments. It was slow, painstaking work, and it required incredible attention to detail. She found it deeply satisfying.

In 1890, Bronya earned her medical degree, one of only three women in her class of more than 1,000 at the Sorbonne. It was now Marie's time to go to France!

However, she was **plagued** by doubt and confusion, even confessing that she had "lost hope of ever becoming anybody." Big sister Bronya wouldn't have it. She told Marie, "You must make something of your life."

And so, at age 24, nearly a decade after finishing high school, Marie set off on a train for the long journey west, to Paris.

ESSENTIAL QUESTION

How did Marie Curie's early environment shape her as a scientist?

In Her Own Words

"To my great joy, I was able, for the first time in my life, to find access to a laboratory. . . . I found little time to work there, except in the evenings and on Sundays, and was generally left to myself. I tried out various experiments described in treatises on physics and chemistry, and the results were sometimes unexpected. At times, I would be encouraged by a little unhoped-for success, at others I would be in the deepest despair because of accidents and failures resulting from my inexperience. But on the whole, though I was taught that the way of progress is neither swift nor easy, this first trial confirmed in me the taste for experimental research in the fields of physics and chemistry."

—Marie Curie

CHEMISTRY KIT
° science journal
° art supplies

BEFORE SHE WAS
MARIE CURIE

You, like Marie, can be a teacher! Make an illustrated book about her early life to share with younger children. Share it with your school's librarian as an addition to the collection!

❯ **Review the information in this chapter about Marie's earliest years.** Jot down key events, ideas, and turning points in your science journal, along with dates.

❯ **Next, make a timeline that plots key events in her early life.** Later, you can include this timeline at the front or back of your book.

❯ **Take a moment to reflect on your notes and timeline.** Based on what you've learned, what do you want your readers to know about Marie's early life? What do you find most interesting about her childhood years? Write a one- or two-sentence summary of your thoughts. If you're stuck, start with three words to describe Marie and her early life and work from there.

❯ **Choose key events and ideas that support the aspects of Marie's life and character you want to explore.** Make an outline in your notebook showing the points about which you want to write and draw.

❯ **Write!** Draw! Remember that the illustrations and text should support each other.

❯ **Assemble your book and be sure to include the timeline.** Staple the pages together or bind with another material, such as ribbon or string.

Think Like Marie!

Don't keep your book to yourself! Share it with family members, classmates, teachers, and librarians!

TEXT TO **WORLD**

How might your home and family influence your own career path?

MEASUREMENTS
MATTER!

Aside from boundless curiosity about the world around them, Marie Curie and Dimitri Mendeleev shared another quality: precision in measurement. Practice your measuring skills with this activity on volume.

❯ **Fill the measuring cup with water to the 2-cup line.**

❯ **Arrange your containers in a row.** Pour the following amounts into each: 2 ounces, 4 ounces, and 10 ounces.

❯ **In your notebook, draw a bar graph showing the different amounts in the three containers.** Beneath each, write the fraction held of the original volume. Then, convert this fraction to a percent. Note the percentage in parenthesis.

❯ **Pour all of the water back into the measuring cup.** Then, redistribute the water equally among your three containers. How many ounces should each hold? Express this number in both ounces and partial cups.

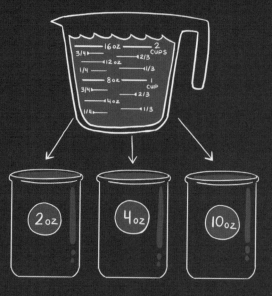

Think Like Marie!

With the help of an adult, experiment with the changing **properties** of matter! Boil your two cups of water. Remove from the stove and let the liquid cool. Pour the cooled water back into your measuring cup. Is the **volume** the same? Next, transform your water into a solid. Pour the water into a freezer bag and place it into your freezer. Remove once it reaches a solid state. Then, let it return to its liquid state at room temperature. Is the volume the same? Record all your observations in your science journal.

WORDS TO KNOW

properties: the unique characteristics of a substance.

volume: a measure of how much space an object occupies.

Chapter 2

DISCOVERING
RADIOACTIVITY

As a young student at the Sorbonne in Paris, Marie Skłodowska stepped into a world that was very different from her native Warsaw. In 1891, Paris was a global capital of culture and science. Its boulevards were lined with bookstores, theaters, and cafes. Here, scientists, artists, and philosophers alike explored the qualities of the substances that make up the world.

ESSENTIAL QUESTION

Why was Marie Curie's discovery of radioactivity so important? How were her scientific investigations a product of her time and place?

Marie was one of the many who came to the city with an interest in examining what was known and how it was represented. What does this mean? It meant questioning every so-called truth that was told to her. It was a world in which examining accepted wisdom was expected and encouraged. As one of her professors urged his students, "Don't trust what people teach you, and above all, what I teach you."

WORDS TO KNOW

advocate: a person who supports another person or a particular cause or policy.

subatomic: the smaller particles inside the atom.

proton: a particle in the nucleus of an atom that has a positive charge.

neutron: a particle in the nucleus of an atom that has no charge.

nucleus: the central part of an atom, made up of protons and neutrons.

electron: a particle in an atom with a negative charge that orbits the nucleus.

A STUDENT'S LIFE

Even though Paris was a completely new environment for Marie—with a new language, customs, and culture—she wasn't alone. She had a guide and **advocate** in her sister, Bronya, who had seven years of Parisian living and a medical degree from the Sorbonne under her belt. Marie's work as a governess had helped finance Bronya's education—now, Bronya and her husband, Kazimierz Dłuski (1855–1930), would repay the favor by providing room and board for Marie.

Do your teachers
**ENCOURAGE
YOU** to
question what
they teach you?

The Smallest Things

The word **atom** comes from the Greek *atomos*, meaning "undivided." For thousands of years, scientists thought that the atom was the smallest unit of matter. But that all changed in the late 1800s and early 1900s. During this period, physicists discovered that atoms were units made up of smaller, **subatomic** particles— **protons** and **neutrons** in the **nucleus**, surrounded by **electrons**.

Check out this fun video explaining atoms and molecules.

🔍 MIT K12 What's all the matter?

Marie Curie in Paris in 1891

Doctor Against the Odds

Marie's older sister, Bronya, born in 1865, earned her medical degree in 1890. Around the same time—a world away on the other side of the Atlantic Ocean—Susan La Flesche Picotte (1865–1918) also defied the social odds to become a doctor.

La Flesche Picotte was born in the Omaha Nation in Nebraska. In 1889, she became the first Native American female doctor in the United States, graduating first in her class at the Women's Medical College of Pennsylvania. Her path to medicine was carved by experience. She decided to pursue this course after seeing a white doctor refuse to treat a Native American woman, who died as a result. After decades as a practicing physician, she opened a hospital in her home community in 1913. It served patients until the 1940s. Today, the historic site is a reminder of her contribution to medicine.

(PS) **Watch this documentary made by students from the Omaha Public School about the Omaha Nation.**

🔍 Omaha Public School Picotte video

In the fall of 1891, Marie set off on an hour-long commute by horse-drawn bus from her sister's home—which doubled as a busy medical practice—to the Sorbonne. Finally, after years of work and waiting, she could register as a student. At last, she would have the chance to devote all of her energy to her studies.

In this new place, she would have the freedom to take whatever courses and attend any lectures she chose.

While she had been using her childhood name, Maria, when it came time to sign the **enrollment card, she wrote the** French version of her name—Marie.

WORDS TO KNOW

expatriate: a person who leaves their country of birth.

pasteurization: a sterilization process developed by Louis Pasteur to remove harmful bacteria from food and drink.

mentorship: when a more experienced person advises and guides a younger person.

This new life wasn't without challenges—the long ride from home to school cut into precious work time. On top of that, a constant stream of guests and a lively, chatty, piano-playing brother-in-law made it quite difficult to concentrate. Finally, living with two other Polish speakers who regularly entertained **expatriates** in their home meant Marie didn't have many opportunities to practice her French.

A few months after arriving, she decided to move to a tiny, sixth-story unheated room in Paris' Latin Quarter. It was low-budget living. On cold winter nights, she slept with all of her clothes piled on top of her to keep warm. But it was closer to school and the laboratories. And, as she wrote her brother, Joseph, the privacy allowed her to work, "a thousand times as hard as at the beginning of my stay."

The Sorbonne in Paris was one of the very few universities in the world THAT ACCEPTED WOMEN. In England, Oxford and Cambridge Universities did not admit women until the 1920s.

The laboratories of Marie and Pierre Curie, the room where electrometrical measurement took place, c. 1900

Credit: Wellcome Collection (CC BY 4.0)

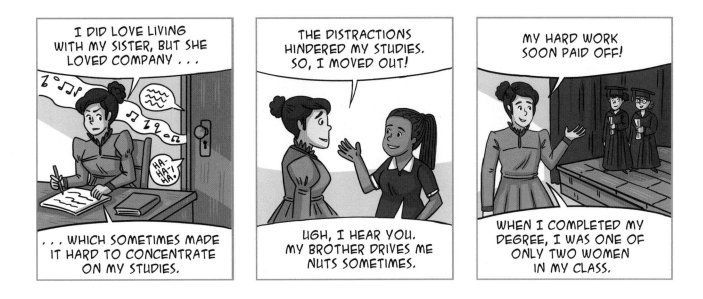

At the Sorbonne, Marie focused on the physical sciences, diving into Mendeleev's periodic table, pondering newly discovered elements, and tackling lab work with a quiet determination. She was there to learn and study—not to socialize. With her gray notebook, she eagerly sat in the front row of every physics lecture, which were led by some of the best minds of her day. Some of these professors saw her potential and originality as a thinker. They offered **mentorship** and, later, research opportunities in their laboratories.

In Marie's day, science was a popular thing to study. The successes of chemist and microbiologist Louis Pasteur (1822–1895), who showed that GERMS CAUSE DISEASE and who developed the process of pasteurization, ensured that the French government supported scientific inquiry by funding it.

In 1893, Marie completed her degree, finishing first in her class. She was one of two women to graduate that year. But her career as a student wasn't over. She had more she wanted to do.

WORDS TO KNOW

feeble-minded: unintelligent.

unconventional: not traditional.

dyslexia: a learning difference that impacts the ability to read and interpret words and letters.

kindred: alike.

With a scholarship allowing her to stay on in Paris for another year, she decided to pursue another degree, in mathematics. She completed that degree in 1894. This time, she finished second in her class. With her pair of honors, she was ready to pack her trunks and head 1,000 miles east, back to Warsaw and her father. But then, a set of forces kept her in Paris.

Where Are the Women?

Whether in lectures or at the lab, Marie was one of only a few female students. While women were allowed to attend the university, there were only 23 women out of a total of 1,825 students. What was it like to be in such a small minority? While her daughter, Ève, later noted that "foreign women were highly regarded at the Sorbonne," the larger culture did not like the idea of women's education and did not believe that women could be leading scientists. Popular books from the time described women as "**feeble-minded**." Women were expected to be accompanied by men in public. For well-born women, the primary "job prospect" was wife and mother. Female scientists were often, as author and historian Barbara Goldsmith notes, represented as masculine, ugly, and unlikely to make significant contributions to the field. How does this differ from points of view held today?

Pierre Curie, c. 1908

First, she got a job offer from the Society for Encouragement of National Industry to study the magnetic properties of various steels. However, she found she needed more lab space. Enter Pierre Curie.

A MEETING OF MINDS

From the moment Marie arrived in Paris, her sister and other Polish expatriates provided security and support. This network of Poles living in and visiting the city pried open the door to one of the key events of Marie's life—meeting Pierre Curie.

When physicist Jozef Wierusz-Kowalski (1866–1927), an acquaintance of Bronya's from Poland, came to Paris on his honeymoon, he learned of Marie's lab space dilemma. Kowalski introduced her to a brilliant young scientist working at the Municipal School of Industrial Physics and Chemistry: Pierre Curie. At a tea hosted by Kowalski, the two connected over their work on magnetism, shared love of scientific precision, and interest in tools of measurement. Pierre helped Marie secure the much-needed lab space at his school, and they continued to see each other.

Even by today's standards, Pierre Curie's early education was unconventional. As a boy, PIERRE STRUGGLED as a student—some biographers think he had dyslexia. Instead of attending a traditional school, he was homeschooled and spent most of his time engaged in hands-on, observation-based learning. These methods worked wonders for him. By the time he was 16 years old, he was studying physics and chemistry at the Sorbonne.

At first, neither Marie nor Pierre were particularly interested in romance—earlier in their lives, neither had been lucky in love. But in each other, they found **kindred** spirits. As Pierre later told many, "We really have the same way of seeing everything."

Still, Marie felt the pull of her homeland, Poland. In the summer of 1894, she returned for a visit with her family with the hopes of getting a job at Krakow University. However, she was denied a position because she was a woman.

WORDS TO KNOW

Enlightenment: a time period in the seventeenth and eighteenth centuries that emphasized reason and science.

While they were apart, Marie and Pierre exchanged pages upon pages of letters. In them, he even offered to pick up his life and work to move to Poland. The pair was in love and found separation impossible. As Marie confessed to a friend, "It is a sorrow to me to have to stay forever in Paris, but what am I to do? Fate has made us deeply attached to each other and we cannot endure the idea of separating."

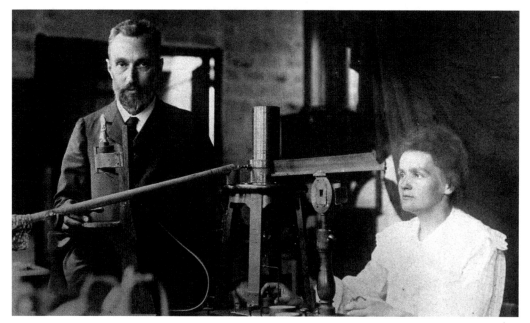

Pierre and Marie Curie in the laboratory, 1904

LOVE AND MARRIAGE

On July 26, 1895, Marie and Pierre made their partnership official by getting married. Marie Curie wore a practical, dark-blue dress to their garden ceremony. She chose it specifically because it could be worn again and again, in the lab. The wedding was followed by a feast and lawn games at the home of Pierre's parents. The couple got a set of new bicycles as a gift and spent the rest of their summer pedaling around the French coast and countryside.

Chemistry's Eighteenth-Century Power Couple

In the bid for science's most famous lovebirds, Marie and Pierre Curie are rivaled by a duo that lived a century before—the Lavoisiers. In 1789, Antoine-Laurent Lavoisier published the *Elementary Treatise of Chemistry*. As the field's first textbook, it brought a revised concept of the elements to curious readers and scientific tinkerers of the **Enlightenment**. Lavoisier's wife, Marie, worked alongside him in his lab, though she was not credited for being his scientific partner. The Lavoisiers' work—and that of rival contemporaries such as Joseph Priestley (1733–1804) in Scotland and Humphry Davy (1778–1829) in England—showed that the ancient elements of air, earth, water, and fire weren't actually indivisible, as people had long thought. These substances could be broken down further. Air actually consisted of oxygen and nitrogen, and water was made of hydrogen and oxygen. Marie also translated key writings from English to French, allowing Antoine-Laurent to stay on top of developments in chemistry on the other side of the English Channel. Marie Lavoisier's drawings, sketches, and lab notes offer a critical window into the tools and processes used by these eighteenth-century trailblazers.

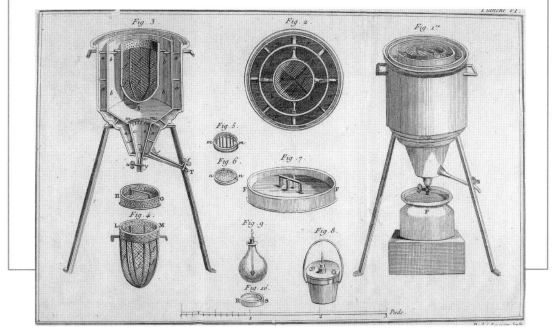

Marie Lavoisier's sketches that appeared in the book, published first in French and then translated into English, *Elements of Chemistry in a New Systematic Order containing All the Modern Discoveries*.

WORDS TO KNOW

PhD: an education degree that shows mastery of a subject.

high-voltage current: the powerful flow of an **electrical charge.**

electrical charge: a property of matter. Protons have a positive charge and electrons have a negative charge.

opaque: something that you cannot see through.

impenetrable: impossible to pass through.

In October of 1895, they returned to Paris. Marie went back to experimenting with steel and Pierre continued teaching, researching, and inventing. Frequently, they'd work side by side. Both night owls, they were known to stay up into the wee hours of the morning, reading until 3 a.m.

Two years later, in September 1897, the Curies welcomed their first child, a daughter named Irène.

Bicycle Craze

In the 1890s, a bicycle craze swept the globe. It was more than just a transportation trend. Cycling became a symbol of women's empowerment, as ladies worldwide traded heavy layers of skirts for bloomers, or loose pants, that made it easier to pedal. One American woman, Annie "Londonderry" Cohen Kopchovsky (1870–1947), embarked upon a 15-month, around-the-world journey by bike. Her tour was widely covered in the popular press and included time in France, where she drew massive crowds of admirers.

The first modern bicycle debuted in the 1880s. By the 1890s, cycling was becoming a popular leisure activity for both men and women.

PS Visit this site to see how the popular press covered Kopchovsky's journey.

🔍 Annie Londonderry

Marie's father-in-law and a hired nurse helped care for the baby, allowing Marie to balance work and motherhood. Soon, she was back in the lab. As she wrapped up her research on magnetism late that year, she set her sights on earning a **PhD**. She scanned publications and journals, looking for an original idea to research and came upon a new and curious topic for investigation.

INVESTIGATING THE INVISIBLE

For Marie, as with all scientists, finding an original research topic was extremely important. She decided to build on a series of discoveries made a few years earlier. She would try to understand and measure the energy of mysterious rays that could travel through solid materials.

This inquiry built on the work of others. It also fit with big questions that others were asking at the time about the nature of matter and the unseen forces that helped drive the form and function of our world.

In the mid-1890s, while studying **high-voltage currents** and using chemicals that glowed under certain types of light, German physicist Wilhelm Conrad Röntgen (1845–1923) discovered a new type of ray. These rays were powerful enough to pass through **opaque** objects, such as wood and human flesh.

"It has become possible to photograph the bones, say, of a human hand without the flesh surrounding the bones appearing on the [photographic] plate."

—report on Röntgen's discovery, published in the *Chicago Tribune*, January 12, 1896

Very dense objects, including bone and metal, were not penetrated by the rays. Instead, an outline image of these **impenetrable** objects was produced.

WORDS TO KNOW

phenomenon: an observable fact or event.

fluorescing: giving off light.

uranium: a naturally occurring radioactive element.

cyanotype: a photographic process that produces a blue-tinted print.

sonification: the use of sound to share information or data.

Röntgen managed to capture this mysterious **phenomenon** on paper in a radiograph. In the first X-ray shared with the world, he captured a photo of the human interior. The image showed his wife's outstretched hand.

In an 1896 paper, he reported on these powerful rays, which he named X-rays, with "X" representing the unknown.

Röntgen won the FIRST NOBEL PRIZE in physics in 1901.

The world was fascinated. In the years following the discovery, 65 percent of papers read at France's Academy of Sciences were written on the topic of X-rays. Pierre suggested that Marie look at a related, but less explored, topic.

In 1896, Henri Becquerel (1852–1908), a physicist working in Paris, had taken an interest in Röntgen's findings. He wanted to see if other substances would emit energy when activated by an external force, such as sunlight. In the process of experimenting, he made an accidental discovery.

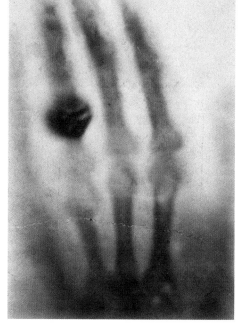

The first X-ray, produced by Wilhelm Conrad Röntgen, showed the hand of his wife, Anna Berthe. On seeing her skeleton, she said, "I have seen my death!"

Here's what happened: Becquerel had planned an experiment that required lots of sun. He would directly expose **fluorescing** crystals—in this case, **uranium** salts—to bright light. Then, he would put them on top of a metal object on an unexposed photographic plate. The effect, he hypothesized, would be a photographic impression from the crystals on the plate.

Science and Photography

Photography was invented in the early part of the nineteenth century. From its beginnings, scientists harnessed this technology to offer new perspectives on the natural world. In the 1840s, British botanical artist Anna Atkins (1799–1871) began using **cyanotypes** to document the structure of plant specimens. With *British Algae: Cyanotype Impressions*, Atkins published the world's first book illustrated by photographs. Atkins placed carefully collected varieties of flowers, feathers, and seaweeds on chemically treated paper. Then, she exposed them to sunlight to produce unique imprints of these items. In the process, she pioneered a process of using photos to show details previously invisible to the human eye. Through these visual records, people could study, explore, and inquire about their environment in new ways. **See these revolutionary images for yourself in this video.**

🔍 world's first photo book

But nature didn't cooperate, and the sun didn't come out. Becquerel's uranium salts—wrapped in black cloth—got tucked into a drawer with the photographic plate and a metal cross. Days later, when he took out the materials to try the experiment again, he came across something surprising.

Even though the items hadn't been exposed to the sun, there was an impression where the metal sat. The uranium salts themselves must naturally emit some kind of energy that allowed for this imprint to happen, he thought.

Today, astronomer Wanda Díaz-Merced, who lost her sight in her early 20s, seeks to make the invisible audible. Díaz-Merced uses **sonification** to study the patterns in stars. Her work has brought art and science together in a music project with the Harvard-Smithsonian Center for Astrophysics. **Listen to the results of this partnership here.**

🔍 X-Ray Hydra original sequence

PS

WORDS TO KNOW

spontaneously: something that happens naturally, without an outside cause.

climate change: a change in long-term weather patterns, which happens through both natural and man-made processes.

carbon dioxide (CO_2): a combination of carbon and oxygen that is formed by the burning of fossil fuels, the rotting of plants and animals, and the breathing out of animals or humans.

atmosphere: the blanket of air surrounding the earth.

greenhouse gas: a gas, such as carbon dioxide, that helps an atmosphere trap and retain heat.

inherent: existing in something as a permanent attribute.

pitchblende: a mineral containing more than 30 elements, including uranium, polonium, and radium.

While others were curious about Becquerel's experiment, few dared to build upon them. Measuring the invisible rays would be a difficult, if not impossible, task.

In taking on this challenge, Curie followed the scientific method, from observation and inquiry to experiment design. First, considering Becquerel's findings, she asked a question: What caused these uranium salts to **spontaneously** emit energetic rays? She set out to make a fundamental study of them, using specialized tools that Pierre and his brother, Jacques, had developed in their study of the electrical charge in quartz crystals.

Uranium was discovered in 1789, MORE THAN 100 YEARS before Curie's experiments. The new element was named after the planet Uranus, the newest known planet in the solar system.

The Birth of Climate Science

In 1896, chemists were just beginning to understand another phenomenon that impacts all life on the planet—**climate change**. Swedish scientist Svante Arrhenius (1859–1927) hypothesized that shifts in **carbon dioxide (CO_2)** had contributed to past changes in earth's temperature. He further proposed that CO_2 emissions from human activity could cause our **atmosphere** to warm in the future. While Arrhenius estimated it would take 1,000 years for a 50 percent rise in CO_2, the earth warmed by 30 percent just in the twentieth century. Today, the effects of **greenhouse gases** on the climate are no longer abstract and invisible. Their toll is measurable in everything from shrinking ice caps to rising surface temperatures. **Watch this short video explaining climate change on Earth.**

🔍 climate change in 60 seconds

In Curie's drafty, damp makeshift lab, she attempted to measure the effect of these salts on the air around them. She found that regardless of their state of matter—liquid, solid, or gas—and temperature, they maintained the same charge. She began to think that it must be something within, rather than outside of, the substance that was creating this energy.

The workroom where Marie Curie conducted her research was a free space at Pierre's school, and it was FAR FROM LUXURIOUS. As her daughter, Ève, later described it, "It was a kind of storeroom, sweating with damp, where unused machines and lumber were put away."

Based on the results of these initial experiments, Curie changed her research question. If uranium salts contained this unchanging charge, do other elements emit a charge that's all their own, too?

She tested samples of each and every known element and found that thorium also emitted a charge. Because these elements seemed to give off an **inherent** radiance, she labeled them "radioactive."

Were there other radioactive substances out there, yet to be identified? Curie tested ore called **pitchblende**, which contained uranium and produced extremely high measures of radioactivity on her electrometer.

It was 1898, and the race was on to identify and isolate these substances locked within the rock.

Pitchblende

ESSENTIAL QUESTION

Why was Marie Curie's discovery of radioactivity so important? How were her scientific investigations a product of her time and place?

ELECTROMAGNETIC SPECTRUM

The mysterious rays that Röntgen, Becquerel, and the Curies studied were forms of electromagnetic (EM) radiation. The **electromagnetic spectrum** consists of seven types of waves of varying lengths, all of which transmit energy and all of which—visible or invisible—constantly bombard us. Use this activity to explore how these forms of EM radiation permeate our everyday life.

> **Head to the library or use the internet to research each type of EM radiation.** From longest to shortest, the wave types are:

1. Radio waves
2. Microwaves
3. Infrared (IR)
4. Visible light
5. Ultraviolet (UV)
6. X-rays
7. Gamma rays

* How long or short are the waves of each type? How is this type of radiation used in your household appliances? In medicine? In communications technology? Find and write down at least one example for each type in your science journal.

> **On seven sheets of paper, note the frequency and the length of each spectrum wave.** Illustrate each card with an example of a form of energy at each point on the spectrum.

> **Using clothespins or paperclips, arrange the cards on a clothesline according to their wavelengths.** Then, arrange them according to frequency. What do you notice?

Think Like Marie!

Take a look at this video on the electromagnetic spectrum. Can you think of any other uses these different types of light might have in the future? How do scientists and engineers brainstorm ideas for applications that haven't ever been thought of before? What does this tell you about the power of innovation?

🔎 Monkeysee ES

WORDS TO KNOW

electromagnetic spectrum: the entire range of radiation that includes high-energy cosmic rays and gamma rays, X-rays, radio waves, short microwaves, ultraviolet and infrared light, and visible light.

MODELING
ATOMIC STRUCTURE

As a chemist, Marie Curie studied known elements and set out to identify new ones. Eventually, she isolated and proved the existence of two—polonium and radium. Today, there are nearly 120 known elements.

When Marie Curie began her career, scientists thought that the atom was the smallest divisible unit of matter. But through her work and that of others who lived at the same time, people learned that atoms consisted of smaller subatomic parts: protons and neutrons at the core, or nucleus, and electrons, which orbited in an outer shell. Each element has a unique profile that depends on its marriage of these miniscule parts.

In this activity, gain a hands-on sense of what lies inside an atom by building a (not-to-scale!) model of a lithium atom.

❯ **Select three colors of gumdrops or marshmallows.** Separate out three of one color, three of another, and four of a third.

❯ **Use toothpicks to connect one of the groups of three with the group of four.** Tightly bunch them. This is your densely packed nucleus that sits at the lithium atom's core! The three gumdrops represent the protons (positive charge). The four gumdrops of the other color represent its neutrons (no charge).

❯ **Attach the remaining three gumdrops to the skewers.** These represent your negatively charged electrons that orbit the atom in its outer layer. Poke these skewers into the nucleus. You've made a model of a stable lithium atom. Why do scientists use models in their work? How do you they help?

Think Like Marie!

Just how small is an atom? View this resource to get a sense of how tiny atoms and their subparticles really are.

🔎 TED Ed atom

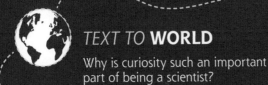

TEXT TO **WORLD**

Why is curiosity such an important part of being a scientist?

Chapter 3

NO SMALL
TASK

Four years of grueling work, with days spent stirring a massive, metal rod in a vat of boiling chemicals. Heavy fumes float up from the tub. The air of the courtyard—or, in bad weather, of the **poorly ventilated** shed bordering it on one side—is thick as the substance in the vat turns from solid, to liquid, to gas.

Why take on this physically taxing, nose-and-throat-searing, incredibly dangerous task?

ESSENTIAL QUESTION

Why was collaboration so important to the Curies?

For Marie and Pierre Curie, the reason was simple—scientific proof. They wanted concrete evidence to show their colleagues and the world that radium existed as a unique, identifiable element.

PROOF IN SPECTRAL LINES

The scientific method was Marie Curie's guide in her quest to figure out what it was in the pitchblende that was emitting rays even more powerful than those of uranium. Observe, question, form a hypothesis, make predictions. Test again and again. Use precise tools of measurement. Record every finding. Analyze the results and develop new questions, hypotheses, and predictions.

Today, we know that ore pitchblende is a complex mineral that consists of MORE THAN 30 ELEMENTS.

Curie's early experiments showed that pitchblende was—in its pure state—about four times more radioactive than uranium. From this, she hypothesized that some other undiscovered element must be hidden in the rock. Pierre paused his own research on crystals to join Marie in her work. Together, the Curies set out to find that mystery element.

The laboratory courtyard of Marie and Pierre Curie, where pitchblende **residue** was distilled, 1900

Credit: Wellcome Collection. Attribution 4.0 International (CC BY 4.0)

WORDS TO KNOW

compound: a substance made up of more than one chemical element.

spectral lines: a unique pattern of lines and colors produced by each element.

spectrometer: a device that analyzes the unique way that each element absorbs and emits light.

prism: an object that disperses light and reflects it into the full color range of the rainbow.

The Curies' research now centered on chemically processing their pitchblende. Their goal was to separate out radioactive **compounds**. They used various methods to analyze the different elements.

Some elements dissolved in acid. The acid could then be poured off, leaving the residue of other elements. This could be tested with an electrometer designed by Pierre that measured the radioactivity emitted by the substance. The Curies could then track and compare the different compounds to get a sense of the compound's footprint.

The results of their experiments showed, as Marie later remembered, "that the radioactivity was concentrated principally in two different chemical fractions." This meant that there were likely not just one but two new elements lurking deep within the pitchblende! But they needed to show the scientific community some kind of visual proof that these new elements were there.

That proof came in the form of **spectral lines**. Each element has its own unique "signature" that can be recorded through a special, telescope-like instrument called a **spectrometer**.

In the years leading up to Marie and Pierre's discovery of polonium and radium, eight other new elements—including helium—had been identified through SPECTROSCOPY.

The spectral lines of polonium, first identified by Marie Curie in 1898

Spectrometers analyze the unique ways that each element absorbs and emits light. Here's how it works. Each substance is heated until it becomes a gas. Then, the light from that gas is examined through a **prism**. The pattern produced will be a distinct set of lines that matches to an element. Curie knew that when she had a pure enough sample, she would see new, previously unseen patterns. But her tests failed, again and again.

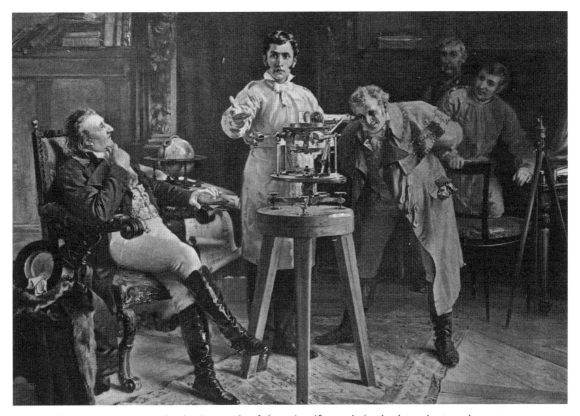

Spectroscopes were intriguing tools of the scientific trade in the late nineteenth century.
Credit: Richard Wimmer, 1897

Finally, in July of 1898, Marie captured the prism's projection of her element's lines. She and Pierre published a paper that introduced the world to their new element—polonium. They also coined the word "radioactivity" to describe its properties. In the paper, they noted that polonium was 400 times more radioactive than uranium.

WORDS TO KNOW

medieval: a period of time between the fall of the Roman Empire and the Renaissance, roughly between the years 350 and 1450. Also known as the Middle Ages.

Renaissance: a cultural movement or rebirth that took place in Europe from the fourteenth through the seventeenth centuries.

optics: an area of physics that studies how light behaves.

atomic weight: the average weight of an atom in an element.

atomic number: the number of protons in an atom's nucleus.

But their work wasn't done. The Curies' experiments hinted that there was another element waiting to be isolated through spectroscopy. In December 1898, they successfully mapped the unique lines that indicated its existence. They named it radium, noting that this new element was 900 times more radioactive than uranium.

"THE ELEMENT IS THERE AND I'VE GOT TO FIND IT!"

Marie and Pierre's accomplishments were heralded by the scientific community. The French Academy awarded her a prize, along with a statement that noted, "The research of Madame Curie deserves the encouragement of the Academy."

Ibn al-Haytham

When and where did the scientific method emerge? In Europe, it first became standard practice during the Enlightenment. Today, textbooks frequently link its development to scholars including Galileo Galilei (1564–1642) or English philosopher Francis Bacon (1561–1626). But its origins actually trace back centuries earlier, to a scientist named Ibn al-Haytham (965–1040) who lived and worked in Egypt. He made major contributions to mathematics, physics, mechanics, philosophy, astronomy, and medicine. As Europe transitioned from the **medieval** period into the **Renaissance**, his work on **optics** was translated from Arabic to Latin. In this and other texts, he described his process of forming a hypothesis and testing it through rigorous experimentation. He showed the world how to do science, influencing countless Renaissance minds, including Leonardo da Vinci (1452–1519), Galileo, and Johannes Kepler (1571–1630).

Marie Curie and her daughters, 1908
Credit: Wellcome Collection. Attribution 4.0 International (CC BY 4.0)

The spectral lines presented convincing evidence of two new elements that would soon take up residence on the periodic table. But other scientists wanted more proof. They wanted a physical sample and a calculable **atomic weight**.

Weight vs. Number

Dimitri Mendeleev organized the periodic table according to atomic weight, or the average mass of one atom in an element. The number essentially equals the number of protons plus neutrons, with a tiny amount of extra weight added by electrons. Based on the findings of physicist Henry Moseley (1887–1915), the table was reorganized by **atomic number**, or the number of protons in a nucleus, in 1913. This became the preferred structure for the periodic table because each element has a whole number attached to it that is both unique and unchanging.

WORDS TO KNOW

alliance: a partnership.

profitable: generating money or income.

patron: someone who lends financial support for a cause.

To obtain the actual substance, they had to overcome a major hurdle. They needed pitchblende, and lots of it. The problem was that pitchblende was expensive. Plus, the mineral was found in only a handful of locations on the European continent, notably in a region under the control of the Austro-Hungarian Empire. This would make it politically difficult to get the substance.

It was a race against time—other scientists were now also working to prove the existence of radium and polonium. The Curies would have to form **alliances** with other scientists and make convincing arguments to get the ore they needed.

Pierre appealed to the Austrian government, asking that they be given the pitchblende

The mine from which the Curies SOURCED THEIR PITCHBLENDE is located in the modern-day Czech Republic.

in the interest of science. Pitchblende was mainly valuable for its uranium deposits, which were used to glaze pottery and in photographic processes. The government agreed to his request, hoping that the pair of chemists would isolate other substances that might be **profitable**.

The space where the Curies treated their pitchblende, 1908

The remaining challenge was transportation. How do you get thousands of pounds of rock from a craggy, Bohemian valley to Paris, a distance of more than 600 miles? Again, Pierre looked to **patrons** of the sciences for help.

The wealthy banker Edmond de Rothschild (1926–1997) anonymously covered the costs. Soon, rail cars brimming with pitchblende crossed from Central to Western Europe. On arrival in Paris, it was dropped by horse carts in the courtyard outside of Marie and Pierre's lab space—which had been previously used for the dissection of dead bodies. Piles of the stuff soon mounded, mixed with pine needles from its mountainous place of origin.

The Nobel Prize-winning chemist **WILHELM OSTWALD (1853–1932) once remarked that the** Curies' workroom was like a "cross between a stable and a potato-cellar."

WORDS TO KNOW

filter: to pass a liquid through something to remove unwanted material.

pulverize: crush.

crystalize: to cause to take a crystallized form, or a highly organized structure.

Now, the Curies had their pitchblende to test. And, despite their shabby lab, they also had countless instruments, some invented by Pierre, to measure their progress.

They decided to focus on isolating radium first, because Marie believed its properties would make it easier to extract than polonium. Still, sifting through the tons of pitchblende for a radium sample was like searching for a needle in a haystack. They divided up the labor, with Marie heading up the chemical and experimental process to find the pure radium salts. At the same time, Pierre looked for the atomic properties of the element. Pierre's school provided a lab assistant. Toward 1900, the school also paid for an aide, a former student named André-Louis Debierne (1874–1949).

During the course of four years, the Curies labored in their lab, working day and night. The intensive process involved boiling 45-pound batches of pitchblende, followed by a complex series of acidic baths to dissolve any salts in the solution. Then, what remained was boiled again. More chemicals were added to this mix. This was **filtered**, **pulverized**, dissolved, and **crystallized**.

Marie and Pierre in their lab, around 1900
Credit: Wellcome Collection. Attribution 4.0 International (CC BY 4.0)

As elements were isolated, they were placed in jars around the lab. As the Curies extracted more and more radioactive substances, these containers lit the damp space with an eerie glow.

The Curies were passionate about their work and grateful for the academy's support of their research, but money continued to be an issue. In 1900, Pierre was offered the chair of physics position at the University of Geneva in Switzerland. The job would come with a better salary, an improved laboratory, and a research role for Marie. For the Curies, it was a tempting proposal, though moving their work would be difficult. But then, the highly respected mathematician Henri Poincaré (1854–1912) helped Pierre land a job at the Sorbonne.

At the same time, Marie got a teaching post at the Normal School for Girls at Sèvres. On top of their tireless quest for radium, along with parenting their

"Sometimes we returned in the evening after dinner for another survey of our domain. Our precious products, for which we had no **shelter, were arranged on tables and boards; from all sides we** could see their slightly **LUMINOUS SILHOUETTES**, and these gleamings, which seemed **SUSPENDED IN THE DARKNESS,** stirred us with ever new emotion and **enchantment."**

—Marie Curie

daughters, they now added full-time work as lecturers. Nonetheless, it gave them the financial security to stay in France. Their research would not have to be interrupted by a move across the Alps.

More good fortune came in the first years of the 1900s. As Marie later noted, their progress had been hampered by a lack of employees. They simply did not have enough people—or enough time—to process all the pitchblende.

Interest in the Curies' discovery was a truly global phenomenon. 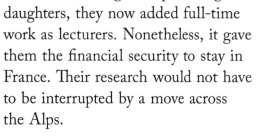 **Read this American newspaper article from 1900 to learn how their early findings were presented to the public.** How does the language in this article differ from newspaper language today?

🔍 Kentucky Crittenden Press "radium"

WORDS TO KNOW

fractionalization: the process of dividing up.

In her autobiography, she wrote, "We found that we could not make further progress without the aid of industrial means of treating our raw material." But they were lucky. Industrial means were found in the form of new employees. A partnership with the Central Society of Chemical Products allowed the Curies to shift some of their labor to trained professionals. Their assistant André-Louis Debierne oversaw this partnership. His pay was now also covered by the Central Society.

The new partnership made the process of distilling the ore much faster. Debierne and his team brought Curie the treated materials. Then, she performed **fractionalizations** and measurements. The radioactivity measures were climbing as the substance became purer. They were getting closer to their hoped-for sample.

The Academy of Sciences recognized this, and in 1902, awarded them 20,000 francs to carry on with their work (approximately $121,000 in current terms). An industrialist who envisioned medical uses for radium also teamed up with the Curies, providing them lab space within his factory.

Closed Doors at France's Academy of Sciences

In the summer of 1898, Marie Curie announced the discovery of polonium to the world. But she herself couldn't deliver news of the success to France's most important group of scientists. Only members of the prestigious academy could deliver papers before their peers, so a former professor presented on her behalf. While Pierre Curie was elected to the Academy of Sciences in 1905, Marie was never allowed to join its ranks. Her application in 1910 was rejected by two votes and resulted in the academy's decision to permanently ban women. Despite French women getting the right to vote in 1944 and making gains in health, education, and work opportunities in the 1960s and 1970s, the academy's policy of exclusion wasn't fully overturned until 1979.

JUST HOW MUCH IS 8 TONS?

The amount equals 16,000 pounds. Consider that one female African elephant—the largest land animal on earth—weighs in between 2 and 3 tons.

With all of this help, they achieved their goal. On March 28, 1902, after processing more than 8 tons of pitchblende, they finally isolated pure radium. While the amount of the substance was miniscule, coming in at $\frac{1}{50}$ of a teaspoon, it was enough to convince the world of radium's existence and to calculate its atomic weight at 225.93. The next steps? Figuring out what to do with it!

ESSENTIAL QUESTION

Why was collaboration so important to the Curies?

GET ELEMENTAL WITH YOUR
BREAKFAST CEREAL

Iron, zinc, copper, potassium, magnesium. They're all elements on the periodic table . . . and there's also a good chance that they're in your breakfast bowl! Why? Elements such as iron aren't produced by the body, but they are vital to its function. Foods such as beef, fruits, vegetables, and nuts provide good iron sources for humans. But sometimes, people don't get the recommended amounts. Breakfast cereals are frequently **fortified** with iron so that people are sure to get enough. Try the following activity to extract the iron from your morning cereal.

> **Pour the cereal into the bowl and run the magnet over the top.** Does the magnet grasp any of the cereal? Why do you think this is?

> **Crush the cereal with your spoon or another kitchen implement (use a mortar and pestle or a potato masher).** Don't stop until it reaches a fine, powdery consistency.

> **Pour the powder on your paper.** Spread it in a thin layer.

> **Run the magnet over the powder.** Are any pieces collected now? If you spot small, black flecks, you've captured some iron.

> **If you're not successful on the first try, keep grinding down your powder!** You may also wish to try again with a stronger magnet. How much iron were you able to collect?

Think Like Marie!

Try the experiment again with another type of cereal. Did you collect more or fewer particles? Check the nutrition labels to see which of the cereals has a higher iron content and compare it against your findings.

TEXT TO WORLD

We often think of scientists as toiling alone for their "eureka moment," when they have a sudden breakthrough. How was the Curies' work different? What does that tell you about jobs in scientific fields?

WORDS TO KNOW

fortified: when certain foods have nutrients added to them.

INSPIRATION THROUGH
OBSERVATION

In the early twentieth century, painter Sonia Delaunay (1885–1975) was fascinated by the light cast by Paris' newly installed electric street lamps. In her *Electric Prisms* (1913–1914) works, Delaunay set out to capture their dazzling, visual effect through **abstract** art.

❯ **Search the internet for an image of Delaunay's "Electric Prisms" paintings.** If possible, print a color copy of one of the works in the series.

✱ Are the colors vibrant and bold or dull and muted? Why do you think she chose these colors?

✱ What shapes and forms repeat in the work? Why do you think this is?

✱ Is there evidence of the artists' "hand" in the painting or are the brushstrokes and lines clean and unnoticeable? Is it clean and tidy or messy?

✱ What do you think Delaunay is trying to say about the quality of light generated by Paris' electric street lamps?

❯ **Think about the technology that you observe and interact with every day, including computers, cell phones, and hybrid or electric cars.** How could you explore it through color, shape, and line? Could you make aspects of it abstract (for example, how a computer shares information over the web or how the electric, gas, and battery elements of a hybrid car operate), as Sonia Delaunay did in her work?

❯ **With another clean sheet of paper and colored pencils, create your own piece of art inspired by the technology that surrounds you!** Why do you choose the materials, colors, shapes, and techniques you use?

Think Like Marie!

Sonia Delaunay was known for her masterful use of a technique called simultaneous contrast. With simultaneous contrast, artists place two colors side-by-side to shape perception. Research this technique online and use your own art materials to experiment with it.

WORDS TO KNOW

abstract: thought or art that is different from reality or actual objects.

DIY
SPECTROSCOPE

In the search for evidence of new elements, the Curies relied on specialized equipment such as the spectroscope. Through spectroscopy, scientists capture the unique pattern of light and color produced by each element. You can think of each element's **spectral profile** as its own signature rainbow. To gain a basic understanding of how this tool works, make your own spectroscope.

CAUTION: Don't gather and heat elements until they reach a gaseous state. That type of work is best reserved for the safety of the chemistry lab.

> Slice a slit in the empty paper towel roll at a 45-degree angle toward the bottom of the tube. Ask an adult for help.

> On the other side of the tube across from the slit, cut a small viewing hole.

> Trace the circumference of the towel roll on the cardboard. Cut out the circle.

> Cut a straight slit across the cardboard circle and tape it to the top of your tube.

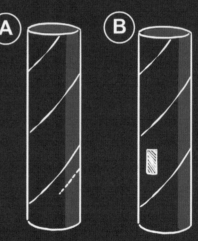

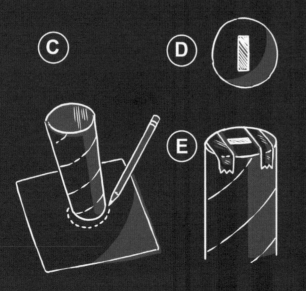

> **Position the CD in the slit at a 45-degree angle with the reflective side up.**

> **Congratulations!** You've made a spectroscope. Test it under different types of light (outdoor, fluorescent, neon, candle) and compare the results. What do you notice? Record your observations in your science journal.

Think Like Marie!

Physicists at the Griffith Observatory in Los Angeles, California, linked spectral lines to "fingerprints of elements in sunlight." What other metaphors do people use to describe something as unique or distinct? How is **figurative language** useful in providing scientific explanations?

Rainbows Are All Around Us

Early spectroscopes relied on prisms to interrupt and bend the movement of visible light. This allowed for a unique band of elemental colors, or spectra, to emerge. But how exactly do prisms break down and separate out the white light that we see?

Here's how it works: Different colors travel at different speeds, with red racing fastest and violet moving slowest. A prism is like an equalizer that bends the light so that we can see the fast, slow, and in-between colors all at once. That process is called **refraction**. Refracting light allows the human eye to perceive all of the colors that it's able to see—red, orange, yellow, green, blue, indigo, violet—at one moment in the magic of a rainbow.

Chapter 4

RADIUM
CRAZE!

The discovery of radium came at the dawn of a new century. To many, the stuff of science fiction that had once been found only on the pages of popular novels by Jules Verne and H.G. Wells seemed to be transforming into science fact. Around the world, radium was declared a "modern marvel." For the general public, radium seemed equal parts wondrous, mysterious, and dangerous.

The world was curious about not just the new element itself—which reporters **speculated** held the power to upend life as it was known—but also about the couple who discovered it. Now the subjects of global curiosity, the lives Marie and Pierre were forever changed. With each honor and award, they had less privacy and were more famous.

ESSENTIAL QUESTION

How did the world respond to the discovery of radium? How did the lives of Marie and Pierre Curie change as a result?

Plus, as they worked more and more with the radioactive substance, their health continued to suffer.

For Marie, radium, which she described as an "infant that I saw being born," and which she contributed to "raising . . . with all my strength," had grown up. Her discovery was now in the world's hands. Try as she might, her control of its destiny was limited. While their discovery paved the way for major scientific gains in understanding the internal structure of the atom, it also triggered a rush toward commercial **exploitation**.

Beyond that, Pierre also foresaw the possibility of radium being "a terrible means of destruction in the hands of criminals who are leading the people toward war." In other words, a weapon.

Given all these developments, in the first decade of the twentieth century, science's first couple aimed to continue to shape the use of this substance that was just beginning to be understood. But factors beyond their own control decided not only radium's path, but also that of their own lives.

Marie Curie's glass beaker that contained the first solution of radium salts. Notice the discoloration of the glass.

Credit: Wellcome Collection. Attribution 4.0 International (CC BY 4.0)

"Radio-activity, the ray-producing property of radium, may be the clew [sic] to the mystery of life and the universe. It may be made to light the streets, run the machines, and do all the WORK WITHOUT EXERTION on the part of men. It has already made blind men see, and is able to destroy microbes and conquer disease."

—*The San Francisco Examiner*, July 5, 1903

WORDS TO KNOW

laureate: a person honored for an outstanding achievement.

conjecture: an opinion formed with incomplete information.

dissertation: a long essay or paper written as a requirement of higher learning, particularly for PhD or doctorate programs.

THE WORLD DISCOVERS THE CURIES

In 1903, the Nobel Prize was a new award. First given in 1901 with funds set aside by Swedish scientist Alfred Nobel, who was best-known as the inventor of dynamite, it honored the finest minds working in their fields with a gold medal and cash prize.

During the first two years, the recipients of the prizes for literature and peace got the most attention. But in its third year, the prize for physics and two of its **laureates**—Marie and Pierre Curie—really captivated the world's attention. Around the world, people wondered: Who was this pair of scientists, partnered in work and in life? What was this mysterious discovery they had made? And how might it be used?

Marie and Pierre Curie's Nobel Prize in physics, won in 1903

Radium on Public Display

Between April 30 and December 1, 1904, the World's Fair drew 19,694,855 visitors to the city of St. Louis, Missouri. Fairgoers marveled at the abilities of the educated horse known as Beautiful Jim Key. They savored the newly introduced ice cream in a waffle cone as they strolled the grounds. They also had the opportunity to listen in on twice-daily lectures on radium offered in the fair's U.S. Government building. As reporter Martha L. Root noted in the July 26, 1904, edition of the *Albuquerque Journal*, each session drew standing-room-only crowds of people who were eager to learn about radium's potential healing properties. Root wrote, "If radium is what some of these scientists **conjecture**, the discovery of radium is second only to the discovery of the law of gravitation." Given that, she proposed that "Mme. Curie, who so logically and brilliantly discovered this new element, should be invited to the World's Fair as its most distinguished guest."

1903 WAS A BIG YEAR FOR CURIE.

In June, she successfully defended her **dissertation and became the first woman awarded a** doctoral degree by the Sorbonne. Later that year, she and Pierre won the Nobel Prize in physics, along with Henri Becquerel (1852–1908), who discovered evidence of radioactivity.

The Curies first received word of a possible Nobel Prize nomination for their study of radioactivity in the summer of 1903. But there was one issue—the nominators put forward Pierre's name alongside that of Henri Becquerel, but not Marie's. Instead, Marie was considered an assistant—someone who simply helped Pierre with lab tasks.

Pierre demanded that this be corrected. The discovery would not have happened without Marie and her achievement had to be recognized. The correction was made, and later that fall, Marie became the first woman to be honored with a Nobel Prize.

WORDS TO KNOW

monetary: having to do with money.

The Curies didn't make the journey to snowy Stockholm, Sweden, for the December 10, 1903, Nobel ceremony. Plagued by pain in his arms and legs, Pierre struggled with everyday tasks and movement. Marie had just suffered a pregnancy loss. They were in no condition to travel. Pierre distracted himself with lecturing, which provided much-needed income, while Marie continued on in the lab.

In the early 1900s, the world was captivated by Marie Curie the scientist *and* Marie Curie the person. **Read this 1907 account from a newspaper in Walla Walla, Washington.** How was her image presented to readers?

🔎 Walla Walla Statesman Curie 1907

Their absence from the ceremony was noted in the press, as was their need for money. As *The New York Times* reported the day after the event, "The discoverers of radium have, it is understood, not profited financially from the work as greatly as might have been expected, and their admirers around the world will be delighted to hear of this windfall for them."

The prize money of $40,000, split with Becquerel, offered a financial cushion. It also paved the way to other **monetary** awards and job opportunities. France granted Marie an additional $12,000 in early 1904 through its Osiris Prize and Pierre secured a full professorship in physics at the Sorbonne—and entry into the Academy of Sciences—in the wake of the Nobel frenzy.

In 1903, the **NOBEL COMMITTEE** awarded prizes in these categories: physics, **chemistry, medicine/ physiology, literature,** and peace. A prize for achievement in economics was added in 1968 and first awarded in 1969.

Marie and Pierre got a lot of press even before the Nobel Prize, but after receiving the award, they catapulted to fame.

In the late nineteenth and early twentieth centuries, newspapers and magazines created a new culture of international celebrity. Readers wanted to know not just about the accomplishments of famous people, but also about their everyday lives. What were their quirks and struggles? What were their habits, wants, and wishes? Were they really, deep down, just like the rest of us?

It would be more than **THREE DECADES** before another woman would win a Nobel in the sciences when Marie Curie's daughter, Irène Joliot-Curie, won in 1935.

The reclusive and media-shy Curies—who "dreamed of living in the wild, quite removed from human beings!"—could no longer escape the prying eyes of a curious public. Their photos were plastered on newspapers in towns as small as Muscatine, Iowa, and as large as London, England.

And the articles didn't always get the facts right. The Curies' lives became retellings of fairy tales and myths. Marie was shown as a poor, Polish Cinderella whose intelligence and passion allowed her to pair up with science's equivalent of Prince Charming. Many news stories about the couple even began with the phrase, "Once upon a time."

WORDS TO KNOW

instability: not dependable or steady.

half-life: the amount of time it takes for half of a reactant to be converted to product in a chemical or nuclear process.

evolution: changing gradually during many years. Humans are believed to have evolved from earlier life forms.

paralysis: the loss of the ability to move.

immune: able to resist a disease or a toxin.

toxic: poisonous, harmful, or deadly.

In pursuit of ever more interesting details, reporters went so far as to break into the family home. Marie reported an incident in a January 22, 1904, letter, explaining that journalists snuck into the house hoping to "report the conversation between my daughter and her nurse, and to describe the black-and-white cat that lives with us."

Pierre also found the attention impossibly distracting from the real work of research. He once called it "the disaster of our lives."

Unpacking the Mysterious New Element

After their Nobel win, Marie and Pierre continued on as relentless researchers. But they weren't the only scientists investigating radium and radioactivity. In the field of medicine, the year 1904 saw the first mention of radium treatment for cancer in a textbook. In physics and chemistry labs across the world, scientists such as Ernest Rutherford (1871–1937) and Albert Einstein (1879–1955) endeavored to understand what was happening inside the atom. Rutherford came to the conclusion that the radioactivity was caused by atomic **instability** and decay. As an element broke down and changed, it produced energy. This process saw one chemical element change into another. Rutherford's research into the **half-lives** of elements, or the amount of time it took them to decay, also showed that rocks and minerals on earth were hundreds of millions of years old. This revolutionary development reset how people thought about the long history of our planet, prior to the **evolution** of human life. Albert Einstein, too, extended Marie and Pierre's research, introducing his theory of relativity in 1905. With it, Einstein hypothesized that tiny amounts of matter could be harnessed to produce massive amounts of energy.

While radium impacted the Curies' privacy, it also directly affected their physical health. Pierre himself noted that extended radium exposure might cause **paralysis** or death and even did animal studies that demonstrated this. But this didn't stop them from working with the new element on a daily basis—and their role as researchers didn't make them **immune** to radium's **toxic** toll.

"Is it right to probe so deeply into Nature's secrets? The question must here **be raised whether it will benefit** mankind, or whether the knowledge will be harmful."

—Pierre Curie

By the time Pierre was 48 years old, the bones in his legs had deteriorated to the extent that he walked with a noticeable limp. On some days, he could hardly stand up. Both Curies also experienced finger pain and numbness as a result of handling radium. Despite the pain and injury, at the end of 1904, the couple welcomed their second child, Ève.

Madame Curie and four of her students, photo taken between 1910 and 1915

Credit: George Grantham Bain Collection (Library of Congress)

WORDS TO KNOW

lesion: a bruise or burn on the skin caused by injury or disease.

ulcer: an open sore on the body.

replicate: to repeat with the same results.

patent: a right given to only one inventor to manufacture, use, or sell an invention for a certain number of years.

huckster: a person who seeks to make profit based on false claims.

luster: a shine.

decay: to break down or to rot.

disfigurement: when part of a body is badly wounded so appearances are changed.

Where in the World?

What country has the most Nobel laureates by population? The tiny Faroe Islands, which lie just four degrees south of the Arctic Circle! Of course, the Faroe Islands have produced only one Nobel laureate, but because there are so few people there, that's a greater percentage than any other country! In 1903, Faroese doctor Niels Ryberg Finsen (1860–1904) won the Nobel in medicine and physiology. In keeping with the trend of the time, his investigations centered on light radiation in treating disease.

RADIUM IN THE WORLD

The idea for medical applications for radium was somewhat accidental. After carrying a vial of the stuff in his jacket pocket, Henri Becquerel noticed burns and sores at the point of contact. Pierre wondered if its effect would be the same on him. He applied a weak dose of radioactive salts to his arm for 10 hours. The result? A **lesion** with **ulcers** that took four months to heal.

The experiment led Pierre to a hypothesis. If radium was powerful enough to destroy healthy skin and tissues, could it be used to kill unhealthy cells? The notion that it could be used to treat certain cancers and other conditions was born. It quickly caught on, and reports of its potential benefits spread.

Because the Curies wanted other researchers to be able to **replicate** their work and make further discoveries, they never **patented** their process for isolating radium. This opened up the door not only for other scientists and medical professionals to explore radioactivity, but also for **hucksters** who hoped to profit from its alleged health effects.

From radium-infused toothpastes to pillowcases to bottled water, radium was touted as a cure for everything from gray hair to sleeplessness. Its glow promised to enhance the appearance of any face and add **luster** to furniture.

WHAT IS RADIOACTIVE DECAY?

Instability in an atom is caused by too many or too **few neutrons. If and when this happens, an atom becomes** radioactive. Radioactive atoms seek balance, so they release energy in order to return to a stable state.

While most products contained only trace amounts of the substance, they still posed a health threat. When consumed or ingested, radium caused bone and tooth **decay**, leading to **disfigurement** and the development of cancer cells. Unfortunately, these hazards were denied for decades, only becoming obvious to the public in the mid- to late-1920s.

A 1918 advertisement for beauty products made from radium. From the turn of the century to the late 1920s, radium was marketed as a beauty elixir and health tonic.

WORDS TO KNOW

spiritualism: the belief system and practices that seek to communicate with the spirits of dead.

seance: a meeting that aims to reawaken and spark communication with spirits.

medium: a person who claims to be able to communicate between the worlds of the living and the dead.

A FATEFUL DAY

Fame and its disruptions, a new child, new jobs, new opportunities, and the world of science pulsing with the details of their discovery—the years 1904 and 1905 were undoubtedly a whirlwind for the Curies. But in April 1906, an event happened that altered the family's life forever.

On April 19, just after the Easter holiday, Pierre was killed in a street accident. It was a rainy afternoon and the cobblestones were slick. As he began to cross a busy intersection, he slipped in front of a horse-drawn wagon and was run over. His skull was crushed under its force and weight.

"His body passed between the feet of the horses without even being touched, and then between the two front wheels of the wagon. A miracle was possible. But the ENORMOUS MASS, dragged on by its weight of six tons, continued for several yards more. The left back wheel encountered a feeble obstacle which it crushed in passing: a forehead, a HUMAN HEAD."

—Ève Curie's description of the accident that killed her father

Later, many people speculated that his radium-weakened bones might have left him unable to dodge the oncoming vehicle.

After Pierre's death, Marie Curie fell into a period of major depression, which she called "the feeling of obsessive distress." She'd lost her life and lab partner. Her daughters felt as thought their mother was as unreachable as their dead father.

The trio moved outside of Paris to be closer to Pierre's father, who along with a nanny, took care of the girls. Curie comforted herself with work, returning to the lab shortly after Pierre's death.

She was committed to honoring their joint legacy by continuing what they'd together started. She kept a journal in which she wrote to him. In it, she wrote, "This laboratory provides me with the illusion that I am holding on to a piece of your life."

Curie carried on Pierre's legacy beyond the laboratory, too, into the Sorbonne's corridors. One month after his death, the science faculty asked Curie to assume her husband's position. She would be the first female professor in the school's 650-year history.

In the fall of that year, she delivered her first lecture to an audience of hundreds of students, journalists, photographers, and academics. Many expected an emotional remembrance of her late husband. But Curie picked up at the precise point where Pierre had left off in his final scientific lecture.

Spiritualism

The direct style with which Marie addressed Pierre in her writings after his death reflected the influence of **spiritualism**. In the early twentieth century, many people dabbled in the supernatural, participating in **seances** guided by **mediums**. The hope was to communicate with the dead. Pierre Curie, in particular, had been interested in the invisible world of spirits and even used scientific tools to measure energy shifts during a seance. Perhaps Marie thought she could meet him again, beyond the boundaries of death.

"For the first time in the long and glorious history of the Sorbonne, we have seen a woman installed as professor. That woman is none other than the distinguished Mme. Curie, so closely associated with her husband in the discovery of that singular substance which has received the name of radium."

—*The Gazette*, Montreal, Canada, November 23, 1906

WORDS TO KNOW

pioneering: the first of its kind.

documentation: a written record of something.

She would honor his legacy on her terms, in her style.

It took years for Marie Curie to feel that balance had been restored to her life. Despite the loss of Pierre, she was remarkably productive. She finished books that he had started and wrote the two-volume *Treatise on Radioactivity*, published in 1910.

In 1909, the Pasteur Institute and the Sorbonne offered to build her a state-of-the-art laboratory, which would become her Radium Institute. On completion, its two divisions would explore the physical properties and biomedical applications of the element. It was to be a **pioneering** space, the only of its kind in France.

Homeschooling, Marie Curie Style

The Curies had a family history of disappointment with traditional schooling. Pierre and his brother didn't learn well in a standard classroom environment and because of this were homeschooled by their father. As Curie's daughters grew up, she became frustrated with their learning options. Along with a handful of other professors at the Sorbonne, she started a homeschooling group made up of about 10 children from six families. It lasted for two years. These lucky kids were taught by the best minds of their day and were even the test subjects for the world's first course on radioactivity! Topics were presented in a hands-on fashion, with games and activities as central to learning. The students also learned Chinese, visited art museums, and engaged in regular physical activity. Can you imagine what it might have been like to go to that kind of school? How is it similar to your own education? How is it different?

A SECOND NOBEL, WITH A SIDE OF SCANDAL

On top of lecturing at the Sorbonne and parenting, Curie continued her work as a chemist. In 1910, she achieved another success—isolating radium as a pure metal. This erased any lingering doubt about the existence of the element. For this accomplishment and for her careful **documentation** of the properties of the radioactive elements polonium and radium, she received a second Nobel Prize in 1911 in the field of chemistry.

But this time, the award was steeped in controversy. In 1910, Curie and a physicist named Paul Langevin (1872–1946) began a romantic relationship. A former student of Pierre's, Langevin was also an unhappily married father of four. Curie and Paul met at a secret apartment, exchanged lengthy letters planning their future together, and even attended conferences together. For the first time in years, Curie seemed to exchange mourning for happiness and hope.

In the autumn of 1911, Marie Curie attended the first Solvay Conference in Brussels. She is seen second from right, seated. Paul Langevin is the figure standing at far right, next to Albert Einstein.

WORDS TO KNOW

nationalism: support for one's own country that often hurts people from other nations.

anti-Semitism: hostility or prejudice against Jewish people.

xenophobia: dislike or prejudice against people from other countries.

justice: fair action or treatment based on the law.

double standard: an ethical or moral code that applies more strictly to one group than to another.

ostracism: being excluded from a group.

duel: a fight between two people with weapons in front of witnesses.

suffragist: an advocate for the right of women to vote.

Langevin's wife, aware of the affair, hired a private detective to steal the couple's love letters. Furious, she released them to the press at roughly the same time the world learned of Curie's second Nobel.

The scandal overshadowed the achievement, as Curie's name was smeared across headlines. She was labeled a foreign-born homewrecker and some even called for her to leave France. Her home was visited by stone-wielding citizens who wanted to shame her for her actions. The Nobel committee went so far as to ask her not to come to Stockholm to accept the award, suggesting that she wouldn't have been given it if the affair had been public knowledge at the time the decision was made.

Nationalism Rising

In the late 1800s and early 1900s, France witnessed a rise in **nationalism**, **anti-Semitism**, and **xenophobia**. After news of her relationship with Paul Langevin broke, the Eastern European Curie was cast as an outsider, a foreign "Other" who corrupted French values. As the American Academy of Physics recounts, the French far right-wing press spread rumors that Curie, "was Jewish, not truly French, and thus undeserving of a seat in the French Academy."

Curie wasn't alone: French Jewish military general Alfred Dreyfus (1859–1935) was falsely accused and convicted of spying in 1894. The ruling against him exposed widespread cultural bias against Jewish people in France. Opinions on the case sharply divided the public. It took more than 10 years for the ruling to be overturned and for Dreyfus to get **justice**.

As a sign of gender **double standards** at the time, Paul Langevin did not face the same degree of **ostracism** and punishment as Curie, despite the fact he was the one who was married. For men in the 1910s, personal issues such as this could be overlooked. For women, they cast a near-permanent shadow. How is this different from today?

In keeping with a standard practice of the era, Paul Langevin CHALLENGED THE PUBLISHER who broke news of the scandal to a duel. While the two men met at the appointed date and time, no shots were actually fired.

Still, Curie had her supporters, including Albert Einstein, who told her to "simply stop reading that drivel." She traveled to Stockholm with her sister, Bronya, and her two daughters. In her December 10 acceptance speech, delivered in French, she noted that the award was not just hers, but also a "tribute paid to the name of Pierre Curie."

She returned to Paris after the ceremony, utterly exhausted and emotionally damaged. She had lost a lot of weight and developed kidney issues. She needed to leave France to rest. She left her children in the care of Polish nannies and went to England, where she was welcomed by scientist and **suffragist** Hertha Ayrton (1854–1923).

Curie stayed in Ayrton's care for nearly a year, returning to France in October 1912. She didn't return to the lab until December of that year. On her reemergence into the world, she was ready to begin launching plans for her Radium Institute.

This multi-year project was lovingly built and finally ready for researchers in August 1914. But a major, global catastrophe would put a pause on that development—and reroute the course of Curie's life—for four more years.

ESSENTIAL QUESTION

How did the world respond to the discovery of radium? How did the lives of Marie and Pierre Curie change as a result?

CHEMISTRY
SCAVENGER HUNT

CHEMISTRY KIT
° science journal
° pencil

From toothpaste to skin creams to bottled water, radium
was found in many personal care and household products
in the early 1900s. While radium has long been retired
from commercial use, many of its neighbors on the periodic table can still be found
on your shelves. After all, elements are the building blocks of everything around us!

❯ Scour your cabinets for everything from fluorine to sodium to zinc! In your science
journal, write the element's name, chemical symbol, and atomic number as your answer to
each clue.

* Element in table salt

* Element added to some toothpastes

* Element found in laundry detergent

* Key (recyclable!) element in many cans
and pans

* Element that powers batteries

* Bananas are high in this element that
regulates blood pressure

* Element behind a coin of the same name

* Liquid metal used in thermometers

* Dairy products such as milk, cheese, and
yogurt are rich in this element

Think Like Marie!

Scientists who work in the field of applied chemistry examine the real world and the
everyday applications and effects of chemicals. An applied chemist might create a
flame-resistant material. They might research the safety of cosmetics, conduct forensic
tests in crime labs, or track the impact of pesticides on humans. Chemists who work
in pure chemistry focus on understanding basic properties and processes of elements
and their bonds. The line between these two related fields can be difficult to draw.
Which of the two do you think the Curies focused on? What makes you think that?

TEXT TO **WORLD**

Can you think of other scientific
discoveries that had both major
drawbacks and benefits?

RADIOACTIVE DECAY

CHEMISTRY KIT

- ° 100 M&Ms
- ° science journal
- ° pencil
- ° plastic cup
- ° cookie sheet or pan
- ° bowl

The term "half-life" refers to the amount of time it takes for half of a radioactive **isotope** to decay, or break down. Isotopes are variants of the same element. Different isotopes of carbon, for example, have the same number of protons, but different numbers of neutrons. Unstable isotopes are radioactive and undergo decay to get back to a stable state. Use M&Ms to visualize this process!

❯ **Count out 100 M&Ms onto the cookie sheet.** Turn the candy pieces so that the "M&M" imprint faces upward.

❯ **In your science journal, make three columns.** Label the first, "Shake," the second, "M&Ms with writing (stable particles)," and the third, "M&Ms without writing (radioactive)." Make seven rows in the "Shake" column.

❯ **For row one, write "100" in the "M&Ms with writing (stable)" column and a "0" in the "M&Ms without writing (radioactive)" column.**

❯ **Place all of the M&Ms in the cup, shake them up, and pour them into the pan.** Examine the M&Ms and remove any without writing and put them in a bowl. These represent your unstable particles that have been shed. Next, count the M&Ms with the writing facing upward. Record both numbers in the designated columns in row two.

❯ **Pour the M&Ms left in the pan back into the plastic cup.** Shake. Again, remove the M&Ms without upward-facing letters.

❯ **Repeat the steps and record your data until your materials have fully "decayed"!**

Think Like Marie!

How many shakes does it take to shed all of the M&Ms? What does that tell you about how long it takes radioactive material to fully decay? How does that contribute to the danger of working with radioactive materials?

WORDS TO KNOW

isotope: a variation in an element based on the number of neutrons. Isotopes of an element have the same number of protons, but different numbers of neutrons.

Chapter 5

HELPING AND
HEALING

June 28, 1914: In a corner of southeastern Europe known as the Balkan Peninsula, conflict erupted between the countries of Serbia and Austria-Hungary. The world held its breath throughout July, waiting to see if a major war could be avoided. But the tension mounted.

By early August, Europe's most powerful countries were divided into two groups: the Allied Powers and the Central Powers. Soon, total war broke out, with much of the world drawn into the bloody conflict. Even in its first month, there were **casualties** due to new, lethal military technologies. By its end in November 1918, World War I claimed the lives of 9.7 million soldiers and more than 10 million civilians. In addition, the number of wounded and missing military service members topped 40 million.

ESSENTIAL QUESTION

How did Marie Curie respond—personally and professionally—to the global catastrophe of World War I?

Many of the world's smartest minds went to work to design, refine, and build the weapons of mass destruction that led to these gruesome outcomes. These ranged from torpedo-equipped submarines that lurked beneath the surface of the ocean to lethal **mustard gas** that quietly crept across battlefields in a yellow haze.

But Curie made a decision: She would not use her scientific expertise to create death and ruin—she would use it to save lives. Rather than develop machines and technologies that could kill, she oversaw the development of a **fleet** of mobile X-ray units for the French military. This technology allowed wounded soldiers to receive better surgical treatments and interventions. In the process, Marie Curie lived up to the motto adopted by her newly completed but yet-to-be-opened Radium Institute, "Science in the Service of Humanity."

World War I began when Austro-Hungarian Archduke Franz Ferdinand and his wife, Sophie, duchess of Hohenberg, were killed in the Bosnian capital of Sarajevo. The killers were part of a militant group that wanted the entire BALKAN PENINSULA LIBERATED from Austro-Hungarian rule.

WORDS TO KNOW

casualties: people killed or injured in battle.

mustard gas: a toxic chemical weapon first used during World War I.

fleet: a group of vehicles.

militant: taking an aggressive or extreme social or political position.

A poster of Madame Curie from 1910

THE RADIUM INSTITUTE ON THE EVE OF WAR

In the spring and summer of 1914, Curie readied every aspect of the Radium Institute, from its state-of-the-art laboratory to the rows of trees and flowers that grew in its gardens. But all that effort was interrupted on August 3, when Germany declared war on France. The institute's work was put on hold, as all but two of its researchers headed for military service on the **Western Front**.

During World War I, fighting happened on two fronts—the Eastern Front and Western Front. The Western Front ran through France and Belgium, stretching more than 400 miles from the North Sea to the Swiss border.

Paris itself was at risk of capture by early September, as the German army marched across Belgium. At this critical, early moment in the war, the city came close to becoming the front line, as the French capital was only 25 miles away from the encroaching forces. The country's panicked government uprooted and moved to a temporary capital in Bordeaux in southwestern France. One-third of the city's civilians, or 1 million people, evacuated the city, Marie Curie's daughters among them.

What do you take with you when you are forced out of your home? As it seemed more and more likely that German troops would seize Paris, Curie sought to protect the institute's most precious resource—the gram of radium in her lab. It was France's entire supply of the important element.

The French government needed money and raw materials, such as metals to make munitions, to finance THE WAR EFFORT. Curie offered her collection of gold medals to officials, but the GESTURE WAS DECLINED. Nonetheless, she invested much of the money from her 1911 Nobel Prize in **war bonds**.

Women in World War I

Marie Curie wasn't the only female scientist who sought to aid the wounded of World War I. The Scottish Women's Hospital at Royaumont in France was staffed entirely by female doctors, nurses, orderlies, administrators, cooks, and technicians. The brainchild of physicians Elsie Inglis (1864–1917) and Frances Ivens (1870–1944), the initial proposal for a women-run hospital was rejected by British military authorities. The French, however, welcomed the medics. The hospital opened in January 1915, operating out of a thirteenth-century **abbey**. It became a model for other relief units across Europe during the course of the war.

Learn more about the Scottish Women's Hospital in this video.

The Scottish Women's Hospital, 1915

🔎 Scottish
Women's
Hospital
YouTube

WORDS TO KNOW

diagnostic: used to determine the identity and cause of an illness or injury.

shrapnel: a fragment of a bomb or shell produced by an explosion.

artillery: large-caliber guns.

Eastern Front: the eastern area of fighting during World War I, between Russia and the east of Germany.

projectile: a weapon that flies through the air.

She packed it in a lead-lined suitcase and boarded a train to Bordeaux. She later confessed that she was "very embarrassed with my heavy bag including the radium protected by lead." She arrived in Bordeaux, stored the radium in a safe-deposit box, turned around, and hopped on an army train headed back to Paris.

Back in Paris, Curie contemplated what she could do to contribute to the war effort. As she later reflected in her *Autobiographical Notes*:

"The dominant duty imposed on every one [sic] at that time was to help the country in whatever way possible during the extreme crisis that we faced. No general instructions to this were given to the members of the University. I therefore sought to discover the most efficient way to do useful work, turning my scientific knowledge to most profit."

How could she use her resources and skills as a scientist to help her country? The answer lay in one of her earliest research interests: X-rays.

A Howitzer gun, used in World War I
Credit: National Library of Scotland

ACTION-ORIENTED

As a scientist, Curie was trained to develop solutions to problems. Just weeks into the war, a major problem became obvious. Military doctors weren't prepared to deal with the massive numbers of wounded men. They also didn't have the **diagnostic** tools they needed to provide accurate treatment. Bullets and **shrapnel** were becoming lodged in the bodies of wounded soldiers. Doctors at the front had to perform painstaking, exploratory surgeries to locate these foreign objects trapped in bone, tissue, and organs, but the process was messy—and painful. With little guidance, military surgeons often had to amputate limbs to save lives. With amputation, the risks became even greater—sometimes, soldiers bled to death from their injuries.

During World War I, combatants on all sides were equipped with high-powered, modern artillery that could shoot **FARTHER, FASTER,** and with **MORE ACCURACY** than in **previous wars. This resulted in an increase in losses. In the first** four months of fighting, there were 5 million casualties on all sides and 1 million deaths.

Curie realized that X-rays would allow physicians to identify the exact location of a bullet or shrapnel. This imaging information would make the hidden interior of a body visible. The **projectiles** would be easier to take out and patients would recover faster and with fewer complications.

The Front Lines

On the other side of the conflict, physicist Lise Meitner also volunteered in the war effort. Meitner was stationed at a military hospital on the **Eastern Front**, where she worked as an X-ray technician and surgical nurse. In an October 14, 1915, letter to a fellow scientist, she described a typical day aiding the wounded of the Austrian army. "I have completed over 200 X-ray films, but that still leaves me much time to help in the surgery room. . . . The gratitude these people feel and show always makes me feel a little ashamed."

But how could you get X-ray equipment, which was heavy to haul and usually housed in specialty hospitals away from the battlefields, to the aid stations on the front line, where they were urgently needed?

The answer lay in pairing X-ray machines with another relatively new technology: the automobile. Curie imagined a fleet of vehicles equipped with X-rays that would allow army medics to be quick, responsive, and able to go where services were most urgently needed. They would be outfitted with an X-ray machine, a darkroom for processing images, and a generator for powering the whole operation. The project would require money, inventiveness, organizational abilities, and a willingness to learn new skills, from how to develop X-rays to how to drive and repair a car.

In the early years of the automobile, women represented a small fraction of **drivers. In the United States in 1910,** JUST 5 PERCENT of people with driver's licenses were women.

Curie was up to the challenge. Within a remarkably short period of time, she managed to see her vision become a reality as director of the Red Cross Radiology Service in France.

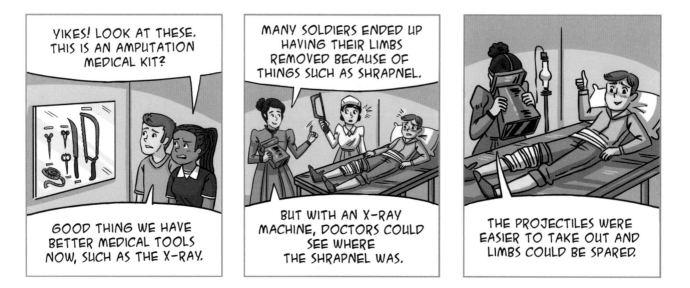

X-ray ambulances near the front in Italy, March 1918

Curie reached out to people she knew—including the Union of Women of France and private donors—to raise money for the fleet. She used her powers of persuasion to convince auto-body shops to convert cars into ambulatory trucks. She lobbied medical suppliers and manufacturers to donate needed parts. And she called on fellow scientists and engineers from the university community to help install equipment.

By late October 1914, the first 20 vehicles were ready to report for duty. These cars were operated by a three-person team. They soon became known on the front as petit Curies, or little Curies.

Curious to see what early X-ray machines looked like? **Take a look at this photo from a World War I base hospital.**

🔎 Base Hospital #28 photo

PS

WORDS TO KNOW

luminescent: glowing.

trenches: a system of long, narrow, open holes dug in the ground, which were used by soldiers during World War I for protection.

Curie's efforts attracted the attention of the media and drew new recruits to her project. Initially, the French military trained soldiers as X-ray technicians. These techs worked alongside physicians, performing and developing the X-rays. But with men constantly moving between areas of engagement, a more stable source of workers was needed.

Each petit Curie was staffed by a three-person team—a physician, an X-ray technician, and a driver. Each member of the trio needed to be ready to assume the tasks of another, in case of accident or injury.

Just months into the war, Curie's 17-year-old daughter, Irène, joined forces with her mother as her radiological assistant. The following year, she graduated to independently directing a radiology unit of her own on the front. The duo went on to train 150 more women to work as technicians through a six- to eight-week course at the Radium Institute, covering everything from radiology to car repair.

Radium Girls

Curie and Irène were routinely exposed to high doses of radiation through their work with X-rays. In the United States, a group of young female laborers unknowingly experienced the ill effects of radium. With men away at the front, women joined the workforce in record numbers to meet wartime production needs. One of those needs was for radium-painted dials for the cockpits of planes. These glow-in-the-dark dials allowed pilots to navigate the night skies. Later, demand surged for **luminescent** watches so that soldiers could keep time in the dark **trenches** where they spent their time.

Girls and women—some as young as 11 years old—were hired by factories in Illinois, Massachusetts, and New Jersey to carry out these delicate painting tasks. The work was intricate, and the brushes were tiny. Workers were encouraged to "lip point," or place the brush in their mouths and wet it with saliva in order to achieve the finest possible tip. As a result, hundreds of employees ingested toxic—sometimes lethal— doses of radium. Damage was often first noted by dentists, who saw an alarming number of young women with tooth and jaw decay. Other ailments followed, including severely weakened bones and cancer.

By the late 1920s, the problem was clear. Five former employees of U.S. Radium sued the company, which continued to deny any danger or wrongdoing. The case made international news. Even Curie commented on it, stating, "I would be only too happy to give any aid that I could, but there is absolutely no means of destroying the substance once it enters the human body." In the end, justice was on the side of the employees. It was a bittersweet victory, but one that paved the way toward laws that protect workers' rights to health and safety in the workplace.

PS Watch a short video clip on the Radium Girls.

🔎 Radium Girls APM

As the lines of the Western Front became established, 200 radiology units were added to Allied field hospitals. Curie oversaw all of these, never hesitating to travel into dangerous combat zones. But the dangers weren't limited to the battlefields. While trained technicians were outfitted with lead aprons to protect them from harmful levels of radiation, Curie and Irène often skipped these safety measures as the need for efficiency was so urgent. Their blood and bones would carry traces of this work for the remainder of their lives and even into death.

A soldier sleeping in a trench
Credit: National Library of Scotland

During the 39 long months that World War I raged, the X-rays that Curie brought to the battlefield were used to examine more than 1 million soldiers. While the technology had been used sparingly in earlier wars because of how hard it was to move, it was now a portable mainstay of treatment. Curie's insistence on making this tool available and bringing it directly to the front saved countless lives.

Always open with her knowledge, she closed out the war years with a book on the subject, *Radiology in War*. Now, doctors and scientists could learn from her experience to help others in times of conflict. That legacy served millions who sought care in crisis zones throughout the twentieth century and even into the present day.

> **ESSENTIAL QUESTION**
>
> How did Marie Curie respond—personally and professionally—to the global catastrophe of World War I?

HOSPITAL HISTORY TRUNK

What did Marie Curie witness on the battlefields of the Western Front at sites such as Verdun? What did she see on her visits to field hospitals? Assemble artifacts th[...] capture the who, what, when, where, why, and how of a medical field hospital in the years 1914–1918, as Curie might have experienced it, to create your own history trunk.

❯ Use the internet or your school or public library to research the medicine of World War I. What types of injuries did soldiers face? What kinds of medical treatment did they receive? Where did they receive treatment? Who was responsible for administering care?

❯ Locate primary source accounts—diaries, newspapers, photographs, X-ray images—that show what conditions were like in field hospitals. Authors can include patients, doctors, nurses, and observers. Print or copy these and add them to your history trunk.

❯ Think about objects that Curie might have seen in hospitals and surgical units, such as bandages, thread for stitching wounds, lanterns, etc. Collect any items available in your house and add them to the box.

❯ Number the objects in the box. Write a guide that explains what each is and how doctors, nurses, and medical technicians used it during the war. Share the artifacts with your family and peers and discuss how medicine has changed during the past century.

"To hate the very id[ea] of war, it ought to [be] sufficient to see on[ce] what I have seen so many times, all thr[ough] those years: men a[nd] boys brought to the advanced ambulan[ce] in a mixture of mud and blood, many of them dying of their injuries, many othe[rs] recovering but slow[ly] through months of pain and suffering."

—Marie C[urie]

Think Like Marie!

During World War I, life wasn't tough just for soldiers in the trenches. Doctors and medics—including Curie—faced major challenges, too. To our modern eyes, the tools they worked with to repair wounded bodies might seem quite primitive. Learn more about the medical equipment used to treat soldiers during the war with this video. What's the same? What's changed?

🔎 BBC WW1

THE TECHNOLOGY OF
WAR

During World War I, engineers and scientists adapted all sorts of new and emerging technologies for the battlefield. Whether by air, underwater, or on land, these developments forever changed the way that war was waged. Choose one of these weapons to research. Then, make a documentary or podcast charting its impact during the War to End All Wars.

❯ **Choose a weapon or technological development from the World War I to research.** Possibilities include:

AIR: Aircraft, zeppelins

SEA: Submarines or U-boats, Dazzle ships

LAND: Armored tanks, machine guns, flamethrowers, barbed wire, poison gas (mustard, chlorine gas)

❯ **Consider the following questions about this technological development.** Use the internet or books from your school or public library to locate reliable resources.

* Who developed it? When and where?

* Why was it developed? Was it always used for military purposes?

* How was it used during the war? Was it used by all sides and on all fronts?

* How destructive was this weapon?

After the threat of a German occupation of Paris lessened, CURIE RETURNED TO BORDEAUX to collect her gram of radium. Back in the lab, she developed radon treatments that could be injected into a soldier's body to destroy damaged tissue.

❯ **Search for primary sources to find what people who lived through World War I thought about this technology.** Your school or public librarian can help you locate documents from organizations such as the Library of Congress or the Imperial War Museum.

TEXT TO **WORLD**

Have you ever had an X-ray taken before? What precautions were in place to make sure you were safe?

WORDS TO KNOW

storyboard: a story mapped out in advance in a series of images.

sniper: a person who shoots from a hidden spot.

- **Think about how you want to tell the story of this technology and its impact on human beings.** Do you have access to images or compelling diary entries or newspaper accounts? Choose whether you want to present it in a documentary film or a podcast, based on the materials that you've located.

- **Write a script in which you make a claim about how this technology shaped the course and outcomes of World War I.** How did it change the way future wars were fought? Be sure to include personal accounts along with data that show its effects. If you're making a documentary, you should also **storyboard** your production, mapping out the images and words in the order they'll appear.

- **Record your documentary or podcast.** Use a movie-making or podcasting platform, such as iMovie, GarageBand, or Soundtrap. Incorporate music from the era for effect. Share it with family, teachers, and peers. Ask them what new details about World War I they learned from viewing or listening to your work.

Henry Moseley

One of the war's many fatalities was Henry Moseley, a British physicist whose work led to the revised periodic table in 1913. When war broke out in 1914, he turned down a professorship at Oxford and took a position as a military officer in the Royal Engineers. He was killed by a **sniper** in Turkey in August 1915. From his research, the periodic table was restructured around atomic number— the number of protons in a nucleus—as opposed to atomic mass, or the weight of the atom.

Think Like Marie!

The fleet of petit Curies that aided troops on Western Front battlefields were made from converted Renault vans. Each makeshift ambulance contained a generator for electricity (powered by the gas engine), a hospital bed, and, of course, X-ray equipment. The windowless carriages also allowed for a darkroom in which X-ray films could be developed. Use a cardboard box, Legos, or other materials at hand to make your own model of a petit Curie that incorporates all of these essential elements.

Chapter 6

GLOBAL
CELEBRITY

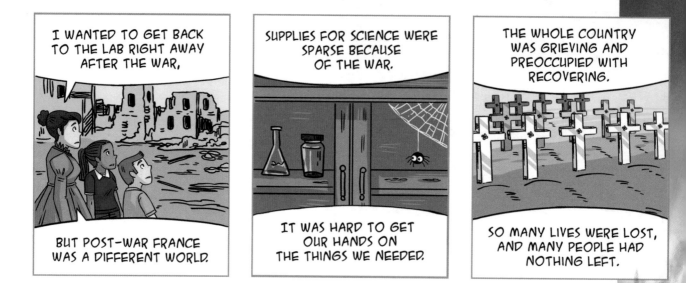

I WANTED TO GET BACK TO THE LAB RIGHT AWAY AFTER THE WAR,

BUT POST-WAR FRANCE WAS A DIFFERENT WORLD.

SUPPLIES FOR SCIENCE WERE SPARSE BECAUSE OF THE WAR.

IT WAS HARD TO GET OUR HANDS ON THE THINGS WE NEEDED.

THE WHOLE COUNTRY WAS GRIEVING AND PREOCCUPIED WITH RECOVERING.

SO MANY LIVES WERE LOST, AND MANY PEOPLE HAD NOTHING LEFT.

After World War I ended in November 1918, Curie was eager to get back to the Radium Institute. She wanted to return to the work of lab life and keep pace with other scientists exploring radioactivity and atomic structure. But the reality of post-war France interfered with this plan.

Human and material resources, such as students and lab researchers as well as funding for the sciences, were in short supply. Given the loss of life and mass ruin caused by the war, the country was grieving.

More than 1.4 million soldiers who fought for France were dead. More than a million others were disabled. Another 2.5 million people found themselves suddenly without fathers and husbands.

ESSENTIAL QUESTION

Why did Madame Curie choose to tour the United States as part of a publicity campaign? Do you think this was a good decision for her?

"Every century has its peculiar field for romance. Sometimes it is the discovery of new lands, sometimes it is war or religion. For us of the 20th century romance has put on the soiled dress of the scientist. The test tube has replaced the sword."

—*The Boston Globe,* May 15, 1921

Cities and towns were destroyed. The countryside was scarred with trenches and littered with shell casings. And immediately after the war, the flu epidemic of 1918–1919 claimed another 450,000 French lives.

In this environment, government funds needed to be used for only the most urgent needs of a distressed society. Scientists, including Curie, would have to wait for better times or look elsewhere for money and resources.

Enter American journalist and editor "Missy" Mattingly Meloney (1878–1943). In May 1920, a mutual friend introduced Curie to Meloney in Paris. Since the Paul Langevin scandal, Curie had avoided the press and eyed reporters with suspicion. But Meloney was different . . . Curie actually liked her.

WORDS TO KNOW

socialite: a person well-known in fashionable society.

ratification: to formally approve or make legal.

She allowed Meloney to interview her for the women's magazine *The Delineator*, which had a readership of 2 million. During that interview, a critical question was asked about what Curie would "most prefer to have in the world." Without hesitation, she answered, "A gram of radium under my own control."

Out of that response, a new partnership was born. One year later, that partnership would bring Marie Curie and her daughters across the Atlantic Ocean to America's shores. There, she would claim a gram of radium financed by America's women.

Mrs. W.B. Meloney, between 1920 and 1925
Credit: Bain News Service

BEFORE THE JOURNEY: A PLAN AND A PROMISE

Why on earth would Marie Curie—who hadn't made a major public appearance for 15 years or given an interview for a decade—agree to meet an American editor, reporter, and **socialite** in the spring of 1920? Perhaps it was a necessity in post-war France, where resources were extremely scarce. Maybe it was the lingering effects of her fondness for the American soldiers who were among her first students at the institute. Or maybe it was that she hoped that Americans would be sympathetic to her cause and use their money and power to help her.

A Changing Political Landscape for American Women

Forty consecutive sessions of the U.S. Congress—from 1880 until 1920—considered the Nineteenth Amendment, which would guarantee women the right to vote. Generations of women fought for its passage, increasingly taking their campaign to the streets in protest marches and parades during the 1910s. During World War I, women also stepped into the labor force in record numbers. As the war raged, women found opportunity to make a new argument in support of expanding suffrage to women: How could Americans fight for the rights of people abroad when the rights of half of its population at home were being denied? That argument—paired with the contributions of women to the war effort—convinced President Woodrow Wilson (1856–1924) to publicly shift his position to support the passage of the Nineteenth Amendment in 1918. On May 21, 1919, the amendment passed the U.S. House of Representatives. Two weeks later, the U.S. Senate followed suit. It then went to the states. On August 18, 1920, the Nineteenth Amendment became the law of the land, when Tennessee lawmakers voted 49-47 in favor of **ratification**.

The National Women's Party picketing the White House, 1917

enfranchised: possessing the right to vote.

humanitarian: a person who works for the public good and to relieve human suffering.

icon: a person who is highly honored and who holds a symbolic stature.

Regardless of the reason, Curie and Meloney met. And met again. They established a friendship. Somehow, during the course of those meetings, they came to an agreement. Curie had a concrete need—radium. This was the key element to advancing her scientific research.

Meloney was a journalist and influencer in America, which had come out of the war as an economic power with an abundant supply of radium. She could help.

At the time of their 1920 interview, France held ONE GRAM of radium. In contrast, the United States held 50 GRAMS.

How would this work? Meloney's plan was to establish a radium fund to raise $100,000 for Curie. After all, in the United States, women had gained suffrage after decades of fighting for it. These newly **enfranchised** women craved success stories about other women. Curie would appeal to career women and young people, doctors' wives, scientists, cancer researchers, and anyone who wanted to support a cause in a country that had plenty of funds for scientific research. That cause, in Meloney's making, would be cancer research.

In this vision, Curie would get a warm-and-fuzzy makeover as a **humanitarian**, a maternal do-gooder who did science not simply because she loved it, but for a greater good.

In today's dollars, $100,000 amounts to $1.3 MILLION!

Curie didn't want to be a symbol. She didn't want to be a political tool or an **icon** who represented selflessness. She just wanted to do science, in her own lab, on her own terms. But she needed radium. She worried about the method, but in the end, agreed to share her story. Her conditions? No mention of the Paul Langevin scandal. When the money was raised, she would travel to the United States with her daughters to claim the radium.

Both women kept their ends of the bargain. Meloney first approached the wives of wealthy businessmen to support the cause with large donations—but was turned down. Then, she went straight to the American public through the pages of her magazine. Within months, the Radium Fund had lots of subscribers, from young girls to college students to professional women.

Meloney had enlisted friends, such as women's movement leader Carrie Chapman Catt (1859–1947) and respected physician Dr. William Mayo (1861–1939), to write articles and editorials to aid the effort. The checks flowed in. Curie, who rarely left France and always traveled under a fake name, would have to leave France—without any disguises—to collect the radium.

"The idea was that the gift would come exclusively from the **AMERICAN WOMEN**. A committee including several prominent women and distinguished scientific men received some **IMPORTANT GIFTS**, and made an appeal for a public subscription, to which a great number of women's organizations, especially colleges and clubs, responded. In many cases gifts came from persons who had **EXPERIENCED THE BENEFIT** of radiumtherapy."

—Marie Curie,
Autobiographical Notes

FRANCE HELD ONLY ONE GRAM OF RADIUM, BUT THE UNITED STATES HAD 50!

WOMEN HAD JUST GAINED THE RIGHT TO VOTE AND WERE LOOKING FOR SUCCESSFUL WOMEN TO EMPOWER.

LUCKILY, BEING IN THE PUBLIC EYE AT THIS TIME HELPED ME OBTAIN THE RADIUM WE NEEDED SO BADLY.

THIS IS WHY IT'S SO IMPORTANT TO SUPPORT EVERYONE, REGARDLESS OF RACE OR GENDER.

EVERYONE SHOULD HAVE A CHANCE AT BEING THE NEXT GREAT MIND!

spectacle: a performance or display.

industrialist: a person who owns and manages large factories.

philanthropist: a person who promotes the welfare of others.

A SIX-WEEK TOUR

On May 4, 1921, a 53-year-old Marie Curie boarded the *USS Olympic* bound for New York. With her were her daughters, Irène, age 23, and Ève, 16. Their arrival on May 11 was—for the attention-shy Curie —an unnecessary media **spectacle**.

Thousands of well-wishers waited from early morning for the three women to disembark. There were Polish delegations and brass bands. Five representatives from the Camp Fire Girls organization eagerly presented Curie with a "red leather bag beaded with a fleur-de-lis design and decorated with the Camp Fire symbol of light in recognition of the light she had given the world." *The New York Times* went along with the newly created story of Curie as a healer, reporting with the headline, "Madame Curie Plans to Cure All Cancers."

The six-week agenda that followed was filled with banquets, lectures, tours, and receptions. Just after the Curies arrived in New York City, they were whisked to a swanky luncheon at the mansion of Andrew Carnegie (1835–1919), **industrialist** and **philanthropist**.

Other special events followed at the Waldorf Astoria, Carnegie Hall, and the American Museum of Natural History, which planned a special exhibit on radium timed to coincide with Curie's visit. The museum also made her the first female fellow in its history.

"Every little while a man or a woman is born to SERVE IN SOME BIG WAY, and such a one is Marie Curie, the discoverer of radium, whose story *The Delineator* publishes this month. Madame Curie is not only great because of her contribution to science, but because of the spirit in which she BESTOWED HER GIFT UPON THE WORLD."

—Missy Meloney writing in the April 1921 issue of *The Delineator*

For Curie, who agreed to the trip on the basis of "the minimum of publicity," this whirlwind must have been quite a shock.

On May 20, Curie's trip reached a high point with a visit to the White House. President Warren Harding (1865–1923) presided over a ceremonial presentation of the hard-won radium. After a brief speech, the president passed Curie a "small golden key opening the casket devised for the transportation of the radium." The radium itself was too valuable and dangerous to pass hands in this setting.

Journalism of Action

Missy Meloney wasn't alone in using the power of the press to fundraise. In 1885, newspaper tycoon Joseph Pulitzer (1847–1911) launched a campaign to save the Statue of Liberty. That year, the statue was sent by France to the United States as a gift . . . on the condition that the United States would provide a pedestal for it to stand on. But the fundraising committee for the statue's base was a flop, and New York's politicians and the U.S. government bowed out of lending aid. Because of this, the towering copper lady had no place to stand when she finally arrived on American soil and her unattached parts actually made their first home in a warehouse!

Enter, Pulitzer. He used the pages of *The New York World* to put out a call for donations from everyday people. With fundraising events—boxing matches, plays, art exhibitions—and sales of mini statues of the copper lady, his idea raised $102,000 (about $2.7 million today) from 125,000 donors. As thanks, he printed each donor's name in *The World*.

Read more about Pulitzer's fundraising success in this article from *The Iola Register*.

🔎 Iola Register statue 1886

WORDS TO KNOW

propaganda: information that promotes a particular perspective or point of view.

BCE: put after a date, BCE stands for Before Common Era and counts years down to zero. CE stands for Common Era and counts years up from zero. This book was published in 2021 CE.

Marie Curie, 1917

Curie endured another month of travel and engagements before setting sail with her precious, radioactive cargo. In that month, she marveled at Niagara Falls and journeyed as far west as the Grand Canyon. More and more, she gave the tasks of lectures and public appearances to her daughters. On a brief stop in Chicago, Illinois—a city with multiple Polish newspapers and more Polish-language speakers than Warsaw—she was greeted with wild adoration.

By mid-June, when she again passed through Chicago, she was under the care of a physician for exhaustion.

The journey finally came to an end on June 28. Curie said goodbye to the United States and again boarded the ocean liner the *USS Olympic* for France. In addition to her radium, she had honorary degrees from Yale, Wellesley, and the University of Chicago. And beyond that prized element valued at $100,000, she had $22,000 worth of other rare metals, $2,000 in prize money, $6,900 in speaking fees, $56,000 in leftover donations from the fund, and a $50,000 advance on her promised autobiography.

The Radium Institute's financial standing was no longer in question.

Curie's Influence

How did American women see Marie Curie? *The Delineator* followed up Curie's visit with an article in its July 1921 issue headlined, "Marie Curie—Through French Eyes." In it, author Stéphane Lauzanne (1874–1958), who connected Curie and Meloney in 1920, made the claim that French women "see in her [Curie] the most startling proof of what woman can accomplish." He continued, "Madame Curie has done for women's rights what a century of **propaganda** and political struggle would not have achieved."

Did Curie really have this effect on women's opportunities in the United States—where she was welcomed by the country's newly enfranchised women? Did she encourage and inspire other women to take up science?

In his speech honoring Marie Curie, President Warren Harding remarked, "We greet you as FOREMOST AMONG SCIENTISTS in the age of science, as **leader among women in the** generation which sees woman come tardily into her own."

While showing that all women could be brilliant scientists was perhaps key to Meloney's agenda, it didn't have the intended effect in the United States. Instead, Marie Curie's tour seemed to cement her status as an outlier and a genius, a person to be admired, but one nearly impossible to imitate. Rather than proving what all women could achieve, the effect centered on honoring what one woman, despite the odds, managed to achieve.

Curie's 1921 visits to selective women's colleges didn't spark a rapid increase in women's admissions to PhD programs in physics and chemistry. Her appearances didn't directly open doors for women interested in working in lab research. In a 1924 survey in which American teenage girls were asked to name their "top heroine," the historically distant Cleopatra—who ruled ancient Egypt from 51 to 30 **BCE**—earned 30 times the votes that Marie Curie did.

While the effort to recast Curie as a kind, cancer-slaying hero may have worked for fundraising, it didn't seem to inspire other women to take up the same career path.

HOME AGAIN

Curie was never shy about stating that her interests didn't lie in politics or in resetting social norms. Instead, her interests were in science for science's sake. When she returned to France, she was happy to go back to work. Throughout the 1920s, money continued to pour in from American donors, allowing work to carry on at the Radium Institute. Because of these funds, the institute operated as a world-class center for research on radioactivity, matched by only a handful of other laboratories in England, Austria, and Germany.

In 1928, a second fundraising effort—this time to raise $50,000 for a gram of radium for a new research center in Curie's native city of Warsaw—was launched, again with Meloney's assistance. In the fall of 1929, Curie sailed once more for America. This time, though, it was all business. At her insistence, there was much less fanfare and far fewer parties.

Marie Curie in a photo taken between 1920 and 1925

Credit: George Grantham Bain Collection (Library of Congress)

The Radium Institute was a site of MAJOR INTELLECTUAL PRODUCTION on the study of radioactivity. **Between 1919 and Curie's death in 1934, scientists** working with the institute published 483 works, 31 of which were authored by Curie herself.

ESSENTIAL QUESTION

Why did Madame Curie choose to tour the United States as part of a publicity campaign? Do you think this was a good decision for her?

UNRAVEL
DNA

In 1920—the same year that Marie Curie met Missy Meloney—future scientist Rosalind Franklin (1920–1958) was born in England. Franklin, an X-ray crystallographer, is best known for capturing the structure of **DNA** on film. Her X-ray image known as "photo 51" allowed scientists to see DNA's double helix spiral and to map its dimensions. Both in and after her short life, she made major contributions to molecular biology.

With this activity, unravel the structure of DNA by making a three-dimensional model of a double helix. The appearance of DNA is often compared to a spiral ladder. The two long strands that would be the ladder's "railings" are connected by "rungs." Each rung is made out of a pair of four chemical bases: cytosine (C), guanine (G), adenine (A) and thymine (T). These don't just match up randomly—as with pieces of a puzzle, A always pairs with T, and C with G.

❯ **Cut a piece of paper into strips that are two feet long and one inch wide.** With your ruler, mark each inch on the strip so you end up with 24 marks.

❯ **Use toothpicks to make the rungs of your ladder.** Pick a color for each base, A, T, C, and G. Take one toothpick and color one half in the color for A, the other in the color for T. Do the same for C and G. Color 10 toothpicks for each pairing.

❯ **Now, make your strand of DNA!** Tape the two paper strips that are your railings together. Poke each toothpick through the lines marking each inch, in any order.

❯ **Once you've placed all 20 toothpicks, gently untape and pull apart the two strips.** It should look like a ladder. Tape the ladder to a surface and twist it until it achieves the spiral structure.

Think Like Marie!

Do some research and discover how the structure of DNA contributes to the way it works. Why are the bases paired like that?

TEXT TO **WORLD**

Have you ever pretended to have a different kind of personality to get something you needed? How did it make you feel?

WORDS TO KNOW

DNA: stands for deoxyribonucleic acid, the substance found in your cells that carries your genes, the genetic information that contains the blueprint of who you are.

MAP CURIE'S
1921 JOURNEY

During Marie Curie's 1921 tour of the United States, she traveled to multiple states and regions of the country. Research Curie's trip to find out just where she went and what she saw.

❯ **When and from what port did Curie depart France?** How long did the journey across the Atlantic take?

❯ **Track as best you can her trip through the country.** Where did she arrive? Where did she go next? Make a calendar marking the city where she was between her arrival on May 11 and departure on June 28. Try to calculate the total miles traveled by Curie and her daughters on this journey.

❯ **Finally, on a world map, visually represent the extent of Curie's travels.** Use pushpins to connect the cities and places she visited.

Missy Meloney with Irène, Marie, and Ève Curie on the 1921 tour

Think Like Marie!

Curie visited Chicago in early June 1921. A report from the *Chicago Tribune* headlined, "Mme. Curie Here, Talks of Lake, Not of Fashions," gives a sense of what captured her attention. The writer explains, "She was besieged by newspaper men and women anxious to get her ideas on the fashions, the war, radium, women's suffrage, the political situation. But the only thing Mme. Curie could talk about was the lake." The author continues, "To her the engineering feat of reversing the flow of the Chicago River . . . was a problem far more interesting than a comparison of American styles with French creations." Why might this have been surprising to audiences? Do you think a rift between fashion and science still exists today?

Chapter 7

AFTER
LIFE

About 100 years ago, crowds of Americans flocked to catch sight of Madame Curie on her first trip to the United States. Today, she still captivates the public, as her story continues to be written and rewritten.

On stage, actors revive the drama of her personal and professional partnerships. An acclaimed, illustrated biography retells her story, tracing its impact on key scientific developments. Her large footprint as the most famous woman in the history of science—often one of the few women represented in her field—has inspired efforts to uncover the stories of lesser-known women in **STEM**.

ESSENTIAL QUESTION

How and why do people's life stories continue to shift, evolve, and change, even after their deaths?

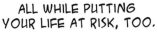

WORDS TO KNOW

STEM: an acronym that stands for science, technology, engineering, and mathematics.

Her continued influence nearly a century after her death begs a couple key questions: What impact did her work leave on the world? What lessons can we learn from her life?

HER FINAL YEARS

Marie Curie spent the last decade of her life directing the Radium Institute in Paris. Here, that precious gram of radium, **crowdfunded** by America's women, led to new experiments and discoveries about radioactivity.

Throughout the 1920s, Irène Curie continued to work alongside her mother at the Radium Institute.

The institute encouraged a Curie legacy that's often forgotten—groups of researchers worked in teams, not as solo scientists. While today Curie is sometimes pictured as a lone genius, this was never the case. She worked with other scientists and assistants, from the early years in the ramshackle lab with Pierre and André Debierne to the Radium Institute days with her daughter, Irène.

Marie Curie knew that progress came faster alongside people who possessed complementary skills. She encouraged others at the institute to collaborate in the same way.

The Beyond Curie Project

In 2017, graphic designer Amanda Phingbodhipakkiya launched the Beyond Curie project. Noting that Marie Curie is all too often the beginning and the end of the conversation about women in STEM, Phingbodhipakkiya set out to introduce the world to lesser-known but equally remarkable female scientists. The objective? To give these "scientists, mathematicians, and engineers who have made incredible advances in their fields" the credit they're due. Today, Beyond Curie features dozens of striking posters that call out the achievements of these hidden figures in science, ranging from Ada Lovelace (1815–1852), the world's first computer programmer, to Chien-Shiung Wu (1912–1997), a physicist who worked on the **Manhattan Project**.

Take a look at some of the cool posters!

🔎 Beyond Curie

Irène and her husband, Jean Frédéric Joliot-Curie (1900–1958), did just that. In January 1934, their research team artificially produced radioactivity when they took the stable element aluminum and made it unstable.

Now with her own partner, Marie Curie's daughter had shown that radioactive elements could be produced in laboratory settings, rather than mined from the earth in an excruciating process. This opened the door for applications ranging from cancer treatments to energy production to nuclear power.

It was a brilliant family legacy for the ailing Marie Curie. She lived long enough to hear about it, but not long enough to see her daughter and son-in-law win the 1935 Nobel Prize for their discovery.

"The results of your researches are of **CAPITAL IMPORTANCE** for pure science, but in addition, physiologists, doctors, and the whole **of suffering humanity hope to gain from your** discoveries, remedies of inestimable value."

—The Nobel Prize in chemistry 1935 award ceremony speech honoring the Joliot-Curies

WORDS TO KNOW

aplastic pernicious anemia: a rare disease in which the body fails to produce enough red blood cells.

martyr: a person who endures great suffering and death for their beliefs.

domino effect: a chain reaction in which one event sets off a series of related events.

subatomic physics: the study of the smallest parts of an atom.

quantum mechanics: the study of how subatomic particles move and interact.

While there are seven parent-child pairs of Nobel Prize winners, THE CURIES REMAIN THE WINNINGEST FAMILY in the history of the award, with five awards spread among Marie and Pierre Curie and the Joliot-Curies.

On July 4, 1934, Marie Curie died of **aplastic pernicious anemia**, an incurable blood disorder caused by long-term radiation exposure. Her younger daughter, Ève, was at her bedside. In obituaries across the world, she was celebrated as a **martyr** to science. Lines from a poem published in *The Boston Globe* on July 9 capture this feeling, which owes much to the image created a decade before by Missy Meloney:

> A little, gray lady,
> Quiet and ever humble . . .
> The pallid face
> Masking the inner flame
> Of inconquerable spirit . . .
> Anybody's mother—
> Yet the healer of
> Millions.

A few years later, Ève Curie wrote a best-selling biography that recounted the span of her mother's life, from birth to death.

A SCIENTIFIC DOMINO EFFECT

Marie Curie lived during a time of major shifts in scientific understanding. She didn't want to just read about these changes in the pages of academic journals—she wanted to play an active role in uncovering new knowledge. Her drive and commitment to finding new ways of knowing—particularly when it came to what couldn't be seen—led to the discovery of radioactivity. The experiments that she and Pierre conducted in their Paris lab helped set in motion the "atomic century."

The drive to understand what was happening inside radioactive elements caused a scientific **domino effect**, leading to breakthroughs in **subatomic physics**, such as the discovery of the proton, a new vision of the atomic nucleus, and remapping of the periodic table. It also paved the way for new applications with a range of positive and negative impacts, from environmentally efficient nuclear power to catastrophically destructive atomic weapons.

Today, members of the Curie family are still important in the world of science. **Watch this interview with Marie's granddaughter, nuclear physicist Hélène Langevin-Joliot (1927–), to learn more about the shaping impact of her family.**

🔎 NEA interview with Dr Hélène Langevin-Joliot

When Marie Curie toured the United States in 1921, she was labeled as a cancer pioneer to make the Radium Fund friendlier to potential donors. While cancer research was never Curie's focus, the potential of radiotherapy as a cancer treatment was considered from the early 1900s.

The First Lady of Physics

Among the scientists who extended Curie's work on radioactivity is one who gained the nickname the "First Lady of Physics." Physicist Chien-Shiung Wu was born in 1912 in Liuhe, China, and she defied the odds of a time and place that forbade girls' education. She went on to graduate from college, earn a PhD at Berkeley, and was the first female professor in the physics department at Princeton. As a Manhattan Project researcher in the 1940s, she came up with new processes for separating uranium. As a professor, her team's findings shattered long-held assumptions about **quantum mechanics**. Despite her work in this area—for which two male colleagues won the Nobel Prize in 1957—she was left out of the honor. Nevertheless, as with Curie, she was a person of many firsts: the first Chinese-American elected into the U.S. National Academy of Sciences, the first female president of the American Physical Society, and the first living scientist with an honorary asteroid in their name (2752 Wu Chien-Shiung).

WORDS TO KNOW

collaboration: working with others.

synthetic radiation: radioactivity that is artificially produced in a laboratory.

feminist: a person who believes men and women should have equal rights and opportunities.

At the Radium Institute's sister organization, the Curie Institute, medical applications for radium were developed by teams of researchers led by Dr. Claudius Regaud (1870–1940). Here again, Curie recognized the value in **collaboration**. With the Joliot-Curies' discovery of **synthetic radiation** in the mid-1930s, the organization's double mission of investigating the properties of radioactivity and looking at medical applications of radium moved even closer together, as artificial radioactivity became a major tool for imaging, diagnosis, and radiotherapy. The two organizations formally merged in 1970.

Today, the Curie Institute remains a major global center for medical research and care. The promise made to American donors 100 years ago to cure cancer has become truer than ever.

The Marie Curie Hospital in London, 1934
Credit: Wellcome Collection. Attribution 4.0 International (CC BY 4.0)

A Final Resting Place

In March 1995, just before his 14 years as president of France drew to an end, François Mitterrand (1916–1996) announced that Marie Curie would be reburied in Paris's Panthéon, the burial site for the country's heroes. The political gesture signaled a cultural shift. In 1993, **feminists** in France had urged the president to honor a woman in this special space, where only men were buried. Two years later, Mitterrand met the request. The Curie family agreed to it on the condition that the bodies of Marie and Pierre remain together in death, as they had in life.

On April 20, 1995, the Curies' remains were moved to their new resting place, making them the 70th and 71st people to be buried in the Panthéon. In a ceremony attended by diplomats, members of the science community, and people from the women's movement, Mitterrand honored Curie's "exemplary struggle" as a "woman who decided to impose her abilities in a society where abilities, intellectual exploration, and public responsibility were reserved for men."

In a country where women then occupied less than 6 percent of seats in parliament and earned 30 percent less than men, Mitterrand's comments honoring Curie were as much about conditions in the present as in the past.

EN 1898

DANS UN LABORATOIRE DE CETTE ÉCOLE

PIERRE ET MARIE CURIE

ASSISTÉS DE

GUSTAVE BEMONT

ONT DÉCOUVERT

LE RADIUM

Credit: Monceau (CC BY 2.0)

WORDS TO KNOW

radiometric dating: a method to determine the numerical age of a rock or fossil. It uses known rates of radioactive decay.

bacteria: tiny organisms that live in animals, plants, soil, and water. Bacteria are decomposers that help decay food. Some bacteria are harmful and others are helpful.

organism: a living thing, such as an animal or a plant.

resilience: the ability to recover quickly from setbacks.

immigrant: a person who moves to a new country to live there permanently.

Curie's scientific footprint spreads even further than the obvious areas of physics and medicine. Seemingly unconnected fields such as earth and food science also have been touched by her legacy.

In 2017, women took a **RECORD 38.7 PERCENT** of parliamentary seats **in France. While the country has made** progress in closing the gender wage gap, men still outearned women by 15.2 percent in 2018.

Radiometric dating, which allows scientists to estimate the age of rocks and minerals, has shown our planet to be far older than nineteenth-century scientists thought. Earth's history, it turns out, reaches back more than 4.5 billion years, long before human development.

The Curies' research findings have also influenced industrial food processing. Today, radiation is used to treat foods to kill **bacteria** and disease-causing **organisms**.

YOU REALLY ARE A KEYSTONE IN SCIENTIFIC HISTORY.

I'M NOT SURE WHERE WE'D BE TODAY IF IT WEREN'T FOR YOUR RESEARCH AND SACRIFICE!

YOUR FINDINGS WERE THE KEY TO MANY OTHER IMPORTANT SCIENTIFIC DISCOVERIES,

FROM ESTIMATING THE AGE OF ROCKS AND MUMMIES TO MAKING SURE WE HAVE SAFE FOOD TO EAT.

THERE IS SO MUCH THAT IS NOW POSSIBLE BECAUSE OF YOU!

MARIE CURIE 1867 -1934

Many of the scientific successes of the twentieth century appear to lead back to the Curies and their discovery of radioactivity.

Marie Curie's story and struggle grew bigger than herself and bigger than the world of science—she has become a symbol of women's achievement and **resilience**. As xenophobia has risen in recent years, she's also been upheld as an icon of **immigrant** success. A permanent exhibit explores her life at the National Center for the History of Immigration in Paris.

Beyond these intellectual, political, and social legacies, Curie's story also continues to inspire artistic productions. From a 1943 Hollywood movie to a 2019 off-Broadway play, this remarkably private woman has kindled creativity across decades.

The tomb of Marie and Pierre Curie at the Panthéon
Credit: TracyElaine (CC BY 2.0)

Often, creative interpretations of Curie's life focus on drama and romance. In recent years, Lauren Redness' acclaimed illustrated biography of the Curies, called *Radioactive: Marie & Pierre Curie, A Tale of Love and Fallout*, was a National Book Award finalist. The book brought Curie back to life not only on the printed page, but also on screen as a 2019 movie. This continued interest in exploring the emotional dimension of her life highlights the timeless qualities of her story—the persistence and brilliance of an underdog in the less-than-welcoming, mostly male world of nineteenth- and early-twentieth-century science.

MEMORIALS AND TRIBUTES aren't limited to Curie's adopted homeland of France. Around the world, there are streets, schools, and playgrounds—such as New York's Marie Curie Playground in Bayside, Queens, which was dedicated in 1956—to honor her legacy.

In Warsaw, the Maria Skłodowska-Curie Museum is located in the apartment building where Curie was born. While other museums feature exhibits in her honor, this is the only institution in the world exclusively devoted to her life and legacy.

Credit: Nihil novi (CC BY 3.0)

An Element in Their Honor

In the mid-1940s, researchers at the University of Chicago and University of California, Berkeley, discovered two new synthetic elements. This pair of tricky elements were so difficult to separate that the lab teams initially dubbed them "**pandemonium**" and "**delirium**." Later, they were named "curium," in honor of Marie and Pierre Curie, and "americium." Surprisingly, curium's introduction to the world came not through a conference paper or press release, but rather on a children's quiz show on November 11, 1945. Glenn Seaborg (1912–1999), one of the lead researchers, was a guest on NBC's *Quiz Kids*. One participant asked if his lab had produced any new elements. Seaborg let slip word of the discoveries, which were to be made public the following week.

NATURE AND NURTURE

Beyond the knowledge and breakthroughs that she ushered into the world, what lessons can we take from the life of Marie Curie? Undoubtedly, Curie was a brilliant scientist who defied the odds of a male-dominated time, place, and profession. But she also had a remarkable support network that nurtured her talents, allowing her to become the scholar she aimed to be. This supportive network of family and peers was a critical resource unavailable to most women in her time.

For every person who tried to pull Curie backward into traditional roles—including the colleague who omitted her name from the 1903 Nobel nomination or the gentlemen of the Academy of Sciences—there were those who pushed her forward. From her parents to her sister, Bronya, to the women of the Flying University, from Pierre to Irène to Missy Meloney, she had countless supporters who urged her to keep on with her life's work. And because of her own remarkable persistence, boundless curiosity, and confidence in her ideas, she did.

Women in Science Searching for Life

Our understanding of astronomy is being rewritten by NASA scientists such as Natalie Batalha. A leader of the Kepler Mission, Batalha's team have used powerful space telescopes to show that hundreds of other planets with conditions that could support life exist in the universe. Just decades earlier, the findings of these researchers would have seemed unbelievable! What other women in science do you know of?

All people are shaped by their environments—those who surround us show us what we can become. In our world today, it's critical to make the networks and support systems that allow for more than the emergence of rare geniuses. These networks must support a whole generation that can envision what is possible and create opportunities for themselves and others.

That spirit of collaboration will pave the way toward the next round of seismic, scientific shifts that will alter our understanding of the universe.

What mystifies you about our world? What sparks your curiosity? **Listen as Dijanna Figueroa, a marine biologist who explores the wonders of the deep sea, shares her advice with teen reporters on achieving your dreams.**

🔎 Dijanna Figueroa interview Cameron

PS

ESSENTIAL QUESTION

How and why do people's life stories continue to shift, evolve, and change, even after their deaths?

TEXT TO **WORLD**

How are your own challenges shaping you as a person?

THE DINNER PARTY

- ° index cards
- ° table, chairs, and tablecloth
- ° plates or other place settings

During a five-year period in the 1970s, artist Judy Chicago (1939–) created an installation called *The Dinner Party*. The piece features 39 place settings at a triangular banquet table, each of which honors an historically significant woman. At its permanent home at the Brooklyn Museum, an additional 999 names of other women from history are etched in the floor beneath the table. They range from figures in prehistory and the ancient world to the present day, with Sacajawea, Sojourner Truth, Empress Theodora of Byzantium, Virginia Woolf, and Susan B. Anthony among the imagined guests.

Explore this website for interesting information of cool women!

🔎 she can stem

❯ **Visit the Nobel Prize site to learn about female recipients of the award.** In addition to Marie Curie, how many women have received this honor? Visit other websites to learn the stories of other women who have changed science.

❯ **Next, research Judy Chicago's *The Dinner Party*.** This work educated and informed viewers about the contributions of women to history. You'll do the same for each woman's contributions to science.

❯ **Choose 10 to 15 women to profile at your table.** Create a place for each one that includes a biographical card explaining who they were, where and when they lived, and what they contributed to their field. Add to each place setting by choosing an item or emblem that represents the figure.

❯ **Invite your family and friends to visit your**

Think Like Marie!

In 2020, three women were honored with Nobel Prizes in the sciences. Emmanuelle Charpentier and Jennifer A. Doudna shared the prize in chemistry for their work in genetics. They were the sixth and seventh women to receive the prize in this field. In physics, the prize went to Andrea M. Ghez, as well as Roger Penrose and Reinhard Genzel. Ghez, whose research focuses on black holes, was the fourth woman to receive a Nobel in physics. **Listen to an interview with Ghez from the Nobel Prize website.**

🔎 Ghez Nobel

abbey: a large church with buildings attached.

abroad: in a foreign country or land.

abstract: thought or art that is different from reality or actual objects.

advocate: a person who supports another person or a particular cause or policy.

alliance: a partnership.

anti-Semitism: hostility or prejudice against Jewish people.

aplastic pernicious anemia: a rare disease in which the body fails to produce enough red blood cells.

aristocratic: of the highest social class or rank.

artillery: large-caliber guns.

atmosphere: the blanket of air surrounding the earth.

atom: a very small piece of matter. Atoms are the tiny building blocks that combine to make up everything in the universe.

atomic mass: the mass, or the amount of physical matter, in an atom.

atomic number: the number of protons in an atom's nucleus.

atomic science: the field of science that studies the structure of atoms, the arrangement of their particles, and how these arrangements can change.

atomic weapon: a powerful weapon that uses the energy released by the splitting of atoms.

atomic weight: the average weight of an atom in an element.

bacteria: tiny organisms that live in animals, plants, soil, and water. Bacteria are decomposers that help decay food. Some bacteria are harmful and others are helpful.

banishment: to send someone away from a country or place as an official punishment.

BCE: put after a date, BCE stands for Before Common Era and counts years down to zero. CE stands for Common Era and counts years up from zero. This book was published in 2021 CE.

biology: the study of life and living things.

cancer: a disease caused by the uncontrolled dividing of abnormal cells in one's body.

carbon dioxide (CO_2): a combination of carbon and oxygen that is formed by the burning of fossil fuels, the rotting of plants and animals, and the breathing out of animals or humans.

casualties: people killed or injured in battle.

chemistry: the science of how atoms and molecules combine to form substances and how those substances interact, combine, and change.

classify: to arrange by groups.

climate change: a change in long-term weather patterns, which happens through both natural and man-made processes.

collaboration: working with others.

compound: a substance made up of more than one chemical element.

conductivity: the measure of how easily a substance, or material, conducts electricity.

conjecture: an opinion formed with incomplete information.

convention: the way things are usually done.

crowdfund: to raise money by appealing to a large number of people, each of whom gives a small amount.

crystalize: to cause to take a crystallized form, or a highly organized structure.

culture: the beliefs and way of life of a group of people, which can include religion, language, art, clothing, food, and holidays.

cyanotype: a photographic process that produces a blue-tinted print.

czar: the leader of imperial Russia.

decay: to break down or to rot.

delirium: confusion and disorientation.

deportation: to send away or expel from a country.

diagnostic: used to determine the identity and cause of an illness or injury.

disfigurement: when part of a body is badly wounded so appearances are changed.

disrupt: to make a major disturbance that interrupts the usual order of things.

dissertation: a long essay or paper written as a requirement of higher learning, particularly for PhD or doctorate programs.

DNA: stands for deoxyribonucleic acid, the substance found in your cells that carries your genes, the genetic information that contains the blueprint of who you are.

documentation: a written record of something.

domino effect: a chain reaction in which one event sets off a series of related events.

double standard: an ethical or moral code that applies more strictly to one group than to another.

duel: a fight between two people with weapons in front of witnesses.

dyslexia: a learning difference that impacts the ability to read and interpret words and letters.

Eastern Front: the eastern area of fighting during World War I, between Russia and the east of Germany.

economics: having to do with the resources and wealth of a country and the material welfare of humankind.

electrical charge: a property of matter. Protons have a positive charge and electrons have a negative charge.

electromagnetic spectrum: the entire range of radiation that includes high-energy cosmic rays and gamma rays, X-rays, radio waves, short microwaves, ultraviolet and infrared light, and visible light.

electron: a particle in an atom with a negative charge that orbits the nucleus.

electroscope: an instrument that detects and measures electricity.

element: a basic substance, such as gold or oxygen, made of only one kind of atom.

enfranchised: possessing the right to vote.

engineering: the use of science, math, and creativity to design and build things.

Enlightenment: a time period in the seventeenth and eighteenth centuries that emphasized reason and science.

ethnic: a group sharing a common national or cultural tradition.

evolution: changing gradually during many years. Humans are believed to have evolved from earlier life forms.

expatriate: a person who leave their country of birth.

exploitation: the process of making use of something to gain as much as possible from it.

feeble-minded: unintelligent.

feminist: a person who believes men and women should have equal rights and opportunities.

figurative language: language that is not literal and that calls to mind an image or association.

filter: to pass a liquid through something to remove unwanted material.

fleet: a group of vehicles.

fluorescing: giving off light.

fortified: when certain foods have nutrients added to them.

fractionalization: the process of dividing up.

geocentrism: the belief, now disproved, that the earth is the center of the solar system.

greenhouse gas: a gas, such as carbon dioxide, that helps an atmosphere trap and retain heat.

half-life: the amount of time it takes for half of a reactant to be converted to product in a chemical or nuclear process.

heliocentrism: the belief that the sun is the center of the solar system.

high-voltage current: the powerful flow of an electrical charge.

huckster: a person who seeks to make profit based on false claims.

humanitarian: a person who works for the public good and to relieve human suffering.

icon: a person who is highly honored and who holds a symbolic stature.

immigrant: a person who moves to a new country to live there permanently.

immune: able to resist a disease or a toxin.

impenetrable: impossible to pass through.

imperial: relating to an empire.

industrialist: a person who owns and manages large factories.

inherent: existing in something as a permanent attribute.

innovative: coming up with new ideas or methods of doing things.

instability: not dependable or steady.

intrepid: fearless or adventurous.

isolate: to separate one thing from another.

isotope: variation in an element based on the number of neutrons. Isotopes of an element have the same number of protons, but different numbers of neutrons.

justice: fair action or treatment based on the law.

kindred: alike.

laureate: a person honored for an outstanding achievement.

legacy: the lasting influence of a person or event.

lesion: a bruise or burn on the skin caused by injury or disease.

luminescent: glowing.

luster: a shine.

Manhattan Project: a project sponsored by the U.S. government to develop the atomic bomb.

martyr: a person who endures great suffering and death for his or her beliefs.

matter: anything that has weight and takes up space. Almost everything is made of matter.

medieval: a period of time between the fall of the Roman Empire and the Renaissance, roughly between the years 350 and 1450. Also known as the Middle Ages.

medium: a person who claims to be able to communicate between the worlds of the living and the dead.

mentorship: when a more experienced person advises and guides a younger person.

militant: taking an aggressive or extreme social or political position.

mineral: a naturally occurring solid found in rocks and in the ground. Rocks are made of minerals. Gold and diamonds are precious minerals.

molecule: a group of atoms bound together. Molecules combine to form matter.

monetary: having to do with money.

mores: the customs and conventions of a community.

mustard gas: a toxic chemical weapon first used during World War I.

nationalism: support for one's own country that often hurts people from other nations.

neutron: a particle in the nucleus of an atom that has no charge.

norm: something that is typical or standard.

nuclear science: the study of atoms.

nucleus: the central part of an atom, made up of protons and neutrons.

opaque: something that you cannot see through.

optics: an area of physics that studies how light behaves.

ore: a naturally occurring mineral that contains metal.

organism: a living thing, such as an animal or a plant.

ostracism: being excluded from a group.

pandemonium: wild and noisy confusion.

paralysis: loss of the ability to move.

pasteurization: a sterilization process developed by Louis Pasteur to remove harmful bacteria from food and drink.

patent: a right given to only one inventor to manufacture, use, or sell an invention for a certain number of years.

patriotism: a feeling of pride for one's country or homeland.

patron: someone who lends financial support for a cause.

periodic table: the chart that shows and organizes all the known elements.

PhD: an education degree that shows mastery of a subject.

phenomenon: an observable fact or event.

philanthropist: a person who promotes the welfare of others.

philosophy: the study of truth, wisdom, the nature of reality, and knowledge.

physicist: a scientist who studies physics.

physics: the study of physical forces, including matter, energy, and motion, and how these forces interact with each other.

pioneering: the first of its kind.

pitchblende: a mineral containing more than 30 elements, including uranium, polonium, and radium.

plagued: deeply troubled.

poorly ventilated: not allowing for fresh air.

positivism: the nineteenth-century philosophy that emphasized the scientific method, logic, and reason.

prism: an object that disperses light and reflects it into the full color range of the rainbow.

profitable: generating money or income.

projectile: a weapon that flies through the air.

propaganda: information that promotes a particular perspective or point of view.

properties: the unique characteristics of a substance.

proton: a particle in the nucleus of an atom that has a positive charge.

pulverize: crush.

quantum mechanics: the study of how subatomic particles move and interact.

radioactivity: the emission of energy in the form of a stream of particles or electromagnetic rays.

radiography: the process of taking radiographs, similar to X-rays, to assist in medical examinations.

radiometric dating: a method to determine the numerical age of a rock or fossil. It uses known rates of radioactive decay.

ratification: to formally approve or make legal.

reactivity: the measure of how easily a substance undergoes a chemical reaction and releases energy.

refraction: to bend a ray of light and make it change direction.

Renaissance: a cultural movement or rebirth that took place in Europe from the fourteenth through the seventeenth centuries.

replicate: to repeat with the same results.

residue: the material that gets left behind.

resilience: the ability to recover quickly from setbacks.

scientific method: the process scientists use to ask questions and do experiments to try to prove their ideas.

seance: a meeting that aims to reawaken and spark communication with spirits.

shrapnel: a fragment of a bomb or shell produced by an explosion.

sniper: a person who shoots from a hidden spot.

social justice: justice in access to wealth, opportunities, and privileges.

socialite: a person well-known in fashionable society.

sociology: the study of human relationships and social problems.

sonification: the use of sound to share information or data.

spectacle: a performance or display.

spectral lines: a unique pattern of lines and colors produced by each element.

spectral profile: the unique pattern of light and color produced by each element.

spectrometer: a device that analyzes the unique way that each element absorbs and emits light.

speculate: to form a theory without solid evidence.

spiritualism: the belief system and practices that seek to communicate with the spirits of dead.

spontaneously: something that happens naturally, without an outside cause.

STEM: an acronym that stands for science, technology, engineering, and mathematics.

stipend: a small salary.

storyboard: a story mapped out in advance in a series of images.

subatomic: the smaller particles inside the atom.

subatomic physics: the study of the smallest parts of an atom.

suffragist: an advocate for the right of women to vote.

synthetic radiation: radioactivity that is artificially produced in a laboratory.

technology: the tools, methods, and systems used to solve a problem or do work.

toxic: poisonous, harmful, or deadly.

trenches: a system of long, narrow, open holes dug in the ground, which were used by soldiers during World War I for protection.

tuberculosis (TB): an infectious bacterial disease that often infects the lungs.

typhus: an often-fatal disease spread by lice, ticks, mites, and fleas.

ulcer: an open sore on the body.

unconventional: not traditional.

uranium: a naturally occurring radioactive element.

vantage point: a place or position showing a view of something.

volume: a measure of how much space an object occupies.

war bond: a debt issued by governments to finance military operations and production in wartime. By buying war bonds, patriotic citizens lend the government money.

Western Front: the western area of fighting during World War I in France and Belgium.

xenophobia: dislike or prejudice against people from other countries.

Metric Conversions

Use this chart to find the metric equivalents to the English measurements in this book. If you need to know a half measurement, divide by two. If you need to know twice the measurement, multiply by two. How do you find a quarter measurement? How do you find three times the measurement?

English	Metric
1 inch	2.5 centimeters
1 foot	30.5 centimeters
1 yard	0.9 meter
1 mile	1.6 kilometers
1 pound	0.5 kilogram
1 teaspoon	5 milliliters
1 tablespoon	15 milliliters
1 cup	237 milliliters

BOOKS

Bodden, Valerie. *Marie Curie: Chemist and Physicist.* Abdo Publishing, 2017.

Conkling, Winifred. *Radioactive!: How Irène Curie and Lise Meitner Revolutionized Science and Changed the World.* Algonquin Young Readers, 2018.

Mooney, Carla. *Chemistry: Investigate the Matter That Makes up Your World.* Nomad Press, 2016.

Swaby, Rachel. *Trailblazers: 33 Women in Science Who Changed the World.* Delacorte Books for Young Readers, 2016.

WEBSITES AND ARTICLES

The Nobel Prize: Women Who Changed Science
nobelprize.org/womenwhochangedscience/stories

Marie Curie and The Science of Radioactivity
history.aip.org/exhibits/curie

Madame Curie's Passion by Julie Des Jardins
smithsonianmag.com/history/madame-curies-passion-74183598

SELECTED BIBLIOGRAPHY

Badash, Lawrence. "Marie Curie: In the Laboratory and on the Battlefield." *Physics Today*, American Institute of Physics, July 1, 2003. physicstoday.scitation.org/doi/10.1063/1.1603078.

Curie, Ève. *Madame Curie: A Biography*. Da Capo, 2001.

Curie, Marie. *Pierre Curie*. Dover Publications, 2013.

Denny, Shawn, et al. "Advisory Committee On Human Radiation Experiments Final Report." *EHSS Welcome*, U.S. Department of Energy, ehss.energy.gov/ohre/roadmap/achre/intro_9_3.html.

Des Jardins, Julie. *American Queenmaker: How Missy Meloney Brought Women into Politics*. Basic Books, 2020.

Des Jardins, Julie. *The Madame Curie Complex: The Hidden History of Women in Science*. Feminist Press, 2013.

Emling, Shelley. *Marie Curie and Her Daughters: The Private Lives of Science's First Family*. Palgrave Macmillan, 2013.

Goldsmith, Barbara. *Obsessive Genius: Marie Curie, a Life in Science*. Weidenfeld & Nicolson, 2004.

"How Can Energy Travel When Matter Doesn't?" *Science Generation*, SERP Institute, 2018, serpmedia.org/scigen/assets/e4t3-wave-motion.pdf.

"Madame Curie's Visit to America." *Science*, vol. 53, no. 1371, 1921, pp. 327–328. *JSTOR*, www.jstor.org/stable/1645136.

Moore, Kate. *Radium Girls*. Simon & Schuster, 2017.

Phingbodhipakkiya, Amanda. *Beyond Curie: A Design Project Celebrating Women in STEM*, www.beyondcurie.com.

Redniss, Lauren. *Radioactive: Marie & Pierre Curie, a Tale of Love & Fallout*. Dey Street Books, 2015.

ESSENTIAL QUESTIONS

Introduction: How does scientific knowledge change through time?

Chapter 1: How did Marie Curie's early environment shape her as a scientist?

Chapter 2: Why was Marie Curie's discovery of radioactivity so important? How were her scientific investigations a product of her time and place?

Chapter 3: Why was collaboration so important to the Curies?

Chapter 4: How did the world respond to the discovery of radium? How did the lives of Marie and Pierre Curie change as a result?

Chapter 5: How did Marie Curie respond—personally and professionally—to the global catastrophe of World War I?

Chapter 6: Why did Madame Curie choose to tour the United States as part of a publicity campaign? Do you think this was a good decision for her?

Chapter 7: How and why do people's life stories continue to shift, evolve, and change, even after their deaths?

RESOURCES

QR CODE GLOSSARY

Page 7: youtube.com/watch?v=P5o S0vaQWXA&feature=youtu.be

Page 10: youtube.com/watch?v=7RXC9GeKUvY

Page 13: vimeo.com/380358906

Page 17: loc.gov/item/2018689366/

Page 24: youtu.be/FsS0nLKoaoo

Page 25: youtube.com/watch?v=BujLp-uvaVs&feature=youtu.be

Page 32: annielondonderry.com/about-annie-londonderry

Page 35: artsandculture.google.com/asset/anna-atkins-and-her-cyanotype-book-james-hennessy-and-brady-haran/dgGyMAqa5BeKPg?hl=en

Page 35: youtube.com/watch?v=L04ZeJKG_Iw&feature=youtu.be

Page 36: youtube.com/watch?v=n 4e5UPu1co0&feature=youtu.be

Page 38: youtube.com/watch?v=m4t7gTmBK3g

Page 39: youtu.be/yQP4UJhNn0I

Page 49: chroniclingamerica.loc.gov/lccn/sn86069457/1900-03-08/ed-1/seq-7/#words=Curie+RADIUM+radium

Page 60: chroniclingamerica.loc.gov/lccn/sn88085421/1907-05-13/ed-1/seq-2/#words=Curie+Marie+Sklodowska

Page 77: youtu.be/txEM4_9ztKY

Page 81: theworldwar.pastperfectonline.com/photo/DE41AEC4-C7C8-4B8A-A299-213734623556

Page 83: youtube.com/watch?v=_QDQJMIYmwM

Page 85: youtu.be/TDeJvYilsig

Page 95: guides.loc.gov/chronicling-america-statue-of-liberty

Page 103: beyondcurie.com

Page 105: youtu.be/_AOQ8os3Pr0

Page 112: youtu.be/D_Uhkrelscl

Page 113: shecanstem.com

Page 113: nobelprize.org/prizes/physics/2020/ghez/interview

INDEX